Temporal order in disturbed reading

Modern approaches to the diagnosis and instruction of multi-handicapped children

7

Temporal order in
disturbed reading

*Developmental and neuropsychological
aspects in normal and reading-retarded
children*

Dirk J. Bakker

*Pedological Institute, Department of
Developmental and Educational Neuropsychology,
Amsterdam, the Netherlands*

*Foreword by A. L. Benton
Professor of psychology and neurology,
University of Iowa, Iowa City, U.S.A.*

1972

Rotterdam University Press

Foreword

Developmental neuropsychology seeks to elucidate the relations between brain and behavior in immature organisms. That these relations have a distinctive character, as compared to the mechanisms operating in adult organisms, has long been recognized. For example, the hemispheric specialization for language which is such a prominent characteristic of cerebral organization in adults is much more limited and subject to greater modification in children. Similarly, the specific behavioral deficits resulting from focal brain damage in adults do not have quite the same neurological meaning in children.

Apart from these theoretical considerations, there is another reason why developmental neuropsychology constitutes a rather different field of inquiry as compared to neuropsychological study of the adult organism. This is its significance for educational disabilities. Among these disabilities, developmental dyslexia is clearly the most important and, while perhaps there has been a tendency to overestimate its prevalence in the population of school children in Western countries, it is surely a major cause of school failure. Yet it must be conceded that, despite decades of study, the causes and essential nature of developmental dyslexia remain obscure and the search for a deeper understanding of this disability continues. Among the various modes of attack on the problem, the neuropsychological approach (i.e., the identification of cerebral mechanisms of perception and cognition, defects in which may underlie specific reading failure) appears at the present time to be a particularly fruitful one.

The series of studies reported by Dr. Dirk Bakker in this monograph exemplifies the neuropsychological approach. Proceeding from the results of previous research which have adduced at least suggestive evidence that both the perception of the temporal order of events and the capacity to integrate information across sensory modalities play a role in learning to read, he has carefully analyzed the relationships between each of these processes and reading skill in both normal and defective readers. His findings indicate that the capacity to identify temporal order is significantly

5

related to reading achievement independently of the influence of intelligence level on both the perceptual and linguistic performances. Moreover, by comparing the performances of kindergarten children (who have not yet learned to read) on temporal order tasks with their *subsequent* reading achievement after one or two years of instruction, he has been able to show that this perceptual ability significantly *predicts* future reading achievement. The importance of the role of sensory integration in this developmental process is indicated by the finding that the capacity to identify the temporal order of combined auditory-visual sequences predicts reading achievement to a somewhat higher degree than does the capacity to perceive the temporal order of events within the visual modality alone.

The empirical findings of this well-designed series of studies have implications both for conceptions of hemispheric specialization of function in children and for the remediation of specific reading disability. It seems clear that the nature of the relationship between temporal order perception and reading is dependent upon the stage of development of the child, particularly with respect to the progressive lateralization of function which occurs during the early years of school childhood. From the practical standpoint, a number of questions regarding the teaching of reading to both normal and disturbed children are raised by the results, e.g., whether the time has not come to individualize reading instruction in terms of the particular stage of development of cerebral organization of a given child. Here particular attention needs to be paid to the evident differences between boys and girls of early school age in respect to rate of cerebral development.

Dr. Bakker's studies constitute an important contribution to our understanding of the perceptual and linguistic processes involved in learning to read and, by implication, of the cerebral substrate underlying the development of reading skills. They will, of course, be of great interest to researchers in the area. I would only add that practical workers in the pedagogical field should also find this monograph of value in planning their educational programs.

Arthur L. Benton

6

Acknowledgements

*'The liberation of which the Gospel
speaks is the deliverance from the very
real power of the "too-late"'*
Popma, 1965, p. 259 (transl.)

To all those who have contributed to the realization of my dissertation I wish to express my gratitude. I am indebted to:
– My promotor Dr. Jan de Wit, Professor of Child Psychology, Free University, Amsterdam, for his stimulating way of discussing the manuscript.
– Dr. Sipke D. Fokkema, Professor of Experimental Psychology, Free University, for his valuable suggestions for improvement.
– The Board and Director of the Pedological Institute for allowing me to work on this project.
– Prof. Pieter J.D. Drenth and his Staff, as well as Headmasters and Staffs of many schools for their assistance during the experimental phases of the investigation. I am particularly grateful to Mr. P. Borgman, Headmaster of the Johannesschool in Amsterdam-Osdorp.

Colleagues of the Pedological Institute and of the Departments Developmental Psychology, Pedology and Special Pedagogics, Free University, have not withheld their criticism from me, especially during informal talks, which I appreciate.

I gladly mention Jan Boeijenga, Han Groenendaal, Niek den Hartog, Jetty Teunissen and René Verschoor.

Thanks are also due to Mrs. Marja Meijer and Miss Ans Snoek for typing the manuscript.

Mrs. Drs. P.M. Aertsen was willing to translate the text.

In those to whom this study is dedicated, I am thanking all who have directed my thoughts and actions. Certainly my parents, my wife and last but not least my children belong to one or both of these categories.

Contents

Introduction

> *'The history of every science reveals that whoever has made progress in it, is increasingly aware of having only just started'*
> Popma, 1965, p. 255 (transl.)

For several years the perception of temporal order has been subject of various investigations at the Research Department of the Pedological Institute in Amsterdam. The experiments are carried out with normal and reading-disturbed children within the scope of investigations into etiological factors in reading-disturbances.*

Temporal order is undeniably an essential moment in the reading process. It is therefore curious that relatively little attention has been paid so far to this factor in the examination of learning- and reading-disturbances. Bannatyne (1966) also points this out when he says 'It is surprising how many teachers and educational authorities who are concerned with verbal processes forget that language is almost entirely an auditory sequencing process, and I would go so far as to say that a specific language disability could be redefined as a specific auditory sequencing disability' (p. 198). Elsewhere Gattegno (1966) underlines the temporal moment in the reading process: 'Mankind has developed writing on plane surfaces but has proposed both horizontal and vertical writing, ordered from right to left or left to right and from top to bottom. But whatever their chosen order, all scripts require that the correct temporal sequence be found before reading takes place' (p. 176).

But what does temporal order actually mean? In the first chapter of this study an attempt is made at locating this concept in a theoretical frame of reference, in which several approaches are distinguished. The second chapter, referring to this frame, deals with the literature on the relation between temporal order perception (TOP) and reading ability. In the subsequent chapters the results of my own research are discussed, and

---

* For a survey of these investigations one is referred to Bakker (1964) and De Wit & Bakker (1971).

11

lead up to the description of a model in which reading disturbances are conceived as functional developmental disturbances.

The study ends in the way it began, viz. with a theoretical analysis of temporal order as a manifestation of time. The particular nature of time appears to have consequences for the neuropsychology of written and spoken language.

I. Temporal order: Frame of reference

All things occur within time. One comes after the other, events follow each other. It is this succession that we are able to experience, perceive and even reflect on.

When reflecting on it, we cannot but think that the succession of events does not take place in an arbitrary way. On the contrary, we discover order, or more precisely a temporal order. This order is manifest in growth for instance. The plant was first a seed. The old man was once a child. There is a relation between then and now, between past and present. The man has something to do with the child he was and the plant cannot be thought apart from the seed. The temporal relation, however, is not necessarily causal by nature: it is day after, not because of the night.

In language, too, succession is clearly present. The phonemes are pronounced after each other and the graphemes are written down after each other. Without order in this succession, however, language is abracadabra.

Many aspects of time have frequently been examined. In psychology this applies to *duration* in particular (Fraisse, 1963; Michon, 1965; Goldstone & Goldfarb, 1966; Orme, 1969; Ornstein, 1969 and Piaget, 1969).

The subject of this study, however, is not the duration but the experience, perception and retention of *temporal order* or *sequence*. Sequence and duration are not unrelated. Take the following events: doctor arrives – interval of half an hour – child is born. The interval of half an hour will probably be experienced as lasting much longer when the sequence of these events is reversed. On the other hand the duration of the interval may influence the perception of the sequence. One can imagine that with an interval of one minute or even less nobody will remember who came first, the doctor or the child, an ignorance that may earn the former a queer reputation.

When studying the developmental psychological literature on temporal

13

order one will discover that research is carried out in two categories. One might think of a test in which the following is done and asked. A high-pitched and a low-pitched tone are presented shortly after each other, and the testee (*S*) is asked which tone he heard first and which one last. Characteristic of another kind of research are such questions as 'which day was yesterday?' The two kinds of research have to do with temporal order: the high-pitched tone comes after the low-pitched one and today after yesterday.

But there are also notable differences. In the former case something from *outside* the person is presented: two tones, i.e. physically qualified entities having a certain temporal relation. The tones and the perceiver are two individualities, so that in this test one may speak of an *inter-individual* relation in which especially the temporal moment of the physical thing (the tone) is object of perception.

'Which day was yesterday?' The person himself has lived through the day that was yesterday. Piaget (1969) therefore speaks here, not unjustly, of 'lived time' (p. X). By posing the question, yesterday is made into an object. One may indeed say so, because yesterday is not 'empty' time, but a day filled with experiences that one visualizes today through reflection. Spier (1953) calls such an image an intentional object. In the present case, in contrast to the example of the two tones, the perceiver and the thing perceived (it is perhaps better to speak of the 'experiencer' and 'the thing experienced') belong to the same category, and so it is possible to speak of an *intra-individual* relation, a relation *within* one and the same individuality.

In psychopathology one often comes upon disturbances in experiencing time (Hugenholtz, 1938, 1959; Van der Horst, 1952; Wallace & Rabin, 1960; Berk, 1965; Cohen, 1967). With certain psychoses time may no longer 'flow', there may be duration without succession. Ten years ago is the same as yesterday or even today. It is obvious that these cases are concerned with a disturbance in experiencing time as an intra-individual relation. The inter-individual perception of time is mostly less or not at all disturbed (see also Benton, Van Allen & Fogel, 1964). Van der Horst (1952) observes that patients with an amnestic syndrome (korsakow) are as a rule able to reproduce series of digits, sentences and the like, whereas they cannot indicate the hour of the day. They have difficulty with intra-individual time, not with inter-individual time. This is different with aphasic and dyslexic patients as will become evident from what follows in this book.

The concepts inter- and intra-individual have a parallel in the methodology of the behavioural sciences. The duration of the tones as well as the

14

interval in between may be shortened and lengthened by experimenter (E) arbitrarily. One deals here with a manageable and therefore experimental variable. But the experience of yesterday and today are dependent on the person and therefore not directly manageable by E. In this case one can speak of behavioural, viz. non-experimental variables.

It is the purpose of this study to deal with temporal order in inter-individual relations.

Rightly a distinction is made between temporal order and succession (Hirsh & Sherrick, 1961). A temporal order or sequence is an ordered succession. With a succession at least two things succeed each other, with an ordered succession one is dealing with at least two *different* things. So the difference between the two is due to the word 'order' which points to a relation – in the present case to a temporal relation – of at least two things. When two *identical* tones are presented with a certain interval it is possible to ask if one or two tones were heard (succession or not), but not which tone was heard first and which one last (temporal order).

The last question can only be answered when *unidentical* tones are presented.

The *explication* of temporal order is not meant to be the same as the *imitation* of it. When a certain rhythmic pattern is tapped out one may ask someone to repeat this. This is imitation. One may also speak of imitation when the tapped-out pattern is repeated by means of words, for instance when –..– is reproduced as 'long short short long'. With imitation one does not explicitly ask for the location of each element in a series.

This is done when a testee (*S*) is asked which place is taken by the digit 2 in the series 3, 4, 2, 7 or just the reverse, which digit was heard in the third place.*

Hirsh & Sherrick state that it is necessary to label the elements of a series in order to be able to indicate a sequence explicitly. This does not seem to be quite correct. One should be able to identify each element separately but that does not imply that each element should have a label. When presenting series of several meaningless figures, it is not even possible to name the elements. For by definition a meaningless figure cannot be labelled. Yet the elements of the series are distinct and consequently they can be identified individually. In order to investigate the perception of series of meaningless figures, one may use a reconstruction method:

---

* Explication and imitation are task variables. It is possible that these two tasks initiate different processes. With imitation of a sequence probably only the component parts of the pattern are coded while with explication the places of these parts also may receive a code. The nature of the codes depends on the nature of the stimuli and the response required (Sanders, 1967). Codes need not be verbal.

after presentation of a series of figures, they are presented once more but now in an arbitrary sequence and *S* is asked to indicate which figure he saw first, which second, etc.

So by means of reconstruction a recognition takes place with the help of nonverbal codes, on the ground of which the temporal sequence can be explicated. Consequently labelling appears not to be a necessary condition for the ability to explicate a temporal order.

In Fig. 1 an attempt is made at rendering diagrammatically what has been said so far about the temporal order concept.

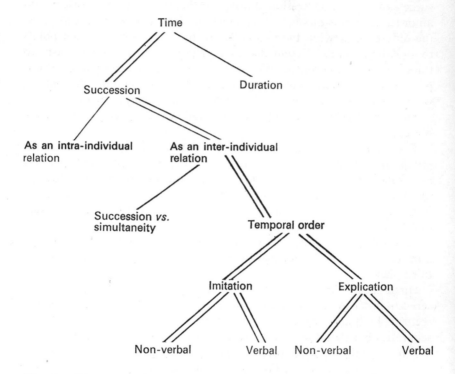

Fig. 1. Lines according to which location of the subject took place. The double lines lead to subjects that are extensively dealt with in this study, and the single lines to subjects that are dealt with less extensively

An example of non-verbal imitation (NI) is the repetition of a rhythmic pattern that has been tapped out. When such a pattern is reproduced by means of words one may speak of verbal imitation (VI). In the case of repeating series of digits as in the WISC we also have to do with verbal

16

imitation. Verbal explication (VE) of a temporal order is required when the location of the digits in such a series has to be mentioned as well. Of non-verbal explication (NE), finally, is spoken when the location of the items in a series of meaningless items has to be indicated by way of a re-construction-method.

II. Temporal order: Relations to written and spoken language

1. INTRODUCTION

Language without temporal succession is no language and language without temporal order is abracadabra. The writing and the pronunciation of a word occurs in temporal succession, but if the word is to be understood, it is essential that there should be an order in this succession. Succession is heard in the pronunciation of sentences such as 'the cork is on the bottle' and 'the rock is on the telbot'. The second sentence is an instance of temporal disorder. Succession is inherent to language, but if language is to be intelligible as in the first sentence the writer or speaker will have to comply with certain rules in respect of the temporal order. The child has to learn these rules.

The spoken word may be written and the written word may be spoken. A child that is able to speak and that is learning to read and write should realize that the sequence of the phonemes correlates to a high degree with the sequence of the graphemes. But there is more involved. Phonemes are things that are heard and graphemes are things that are seen. Moreover, phonemes are ordered in time and graphemes are ordered in space. The child should therefore understand that there is a visual-spatial equivalent of the auditory-temporal structure of a word.

With the actual reading of a word the written word is given. During reading visual-spatial configurations are transformed into auditory-temporal configurations. During writing just the reverse occurs. Here the spoken word is given, i.e. an auditory-temporal pattern. Both during reading and during writing transformations take place, but there is difference in direction.

It is evident that the perception and the retention of temporal order are important moments in the process of learning to read and to write. When a child hears the word 'cork' and writes it down he will put down the 'c' first. For this is the *first* letter of the word. With the term 'first' the temporal moment in the writing process has been illustrated. In the reading-aloud

18

process something similar happens. When a child gets the word 'cork' in print before him and reads it out the [k]-sound is heard first. The phonemes of a word or a sentence read aloud appear in an ordered temporal succession, or in short in a temporal order.

As was remarked in the introduction there are not very many studies on the relation between temporal order perception (TOP) and reading ability. This is rather curious in view of the temporal moment in the learning-to-read process. Add to this that the investigations which are relevant do not always raise the question of the relation between TOP and reading explicitly. Moreover the temporal order concept is often made operational in different ways by various authors.

In the following sections an exposition will be given of recent literature on the relation between TOP and reading. A few studies on the relation between TOP and spoken language will also be reviewed. In this study we will follow the scheme shown in Fig. 1 (Ch. I). This scheme indicates that temporal orders can be reproduced by imitation and explication and in both cases verbally as well as non verbally.

2. NONVERBAL IMITATION (NI) STUDIES

The imitation of tapped-out patterns is a task that belongs typically to the category of NI-studies. The experimenter (E) taps out a rhythmic pattern and S repeats this.

DeHirsch, Jansky & Langford (1966) have included this procedure as a test in their battery for the prediction of reading failures. They found that the results of the test at nursery-school age correlate significantly with reading ability two years later. But on closer inspection of the data, it appeared to apply to girls only.

Some years earlier Stamback (1951) had demonstrated that reading-disturbed children of 7 to 14 years old achieve considerably less than normal readers when imitating rhythmic patterns. Moreover it appeared that the achievements of dyslexic children did not improve with increasing age as opposed to those of normal children.

Recently Blank, Weider & Bridger (1968) carried out a rhythmic pattern test with normal and reading-disturbed children of 6 to 7 years old. These authors found no differences between the two groups, a result that definitely does not fit in with Stamback's conclusion.

Blank et al. did not fail to see this either. They state, however, that the Ss of Stamback used a verbal medium in the performance of their task.

19

Stamback does not give a detailed description of the procedure of the test. But a hint at the rightness of Blank *et al.* may be found in Stamback's remark (p. 483) that the Ss were trained in discerning long and short intervals within the rhythmic patterns.

It is possible that this training was done by means of words and that these words continued to play their part during the test-phase. It is also possible that the difference found by Stamback between reading-disturbed and normal children is only seemingly true. For nowhere in her study is mention made of the groups of readers being matched on IQ. If matching on this variable really did not take place the difference between the two groups is probably less due to a difference in reading ability than to a difference in IQ. From a study by Furth & Youniss (1967), to be discussed later, it appears that intelligence is definitely related to the perception and reproduction of nonverbal temporal series.

In short, we must state that the few nonverbal imitation studies which we are acquainted with do not answer the question of the existence of a TOP-reading relation decisively.

The remark of Blank *et al.* intended for Stamback suggests, however, that a TOP-reading relation may be expected in studies dealing with verbal imitation.

3. VERBAL IMITATION (VI) STUDIES

Temporal order perception in the sense of verbal imitation has, especially in the last few years, frequently been investigated. This does not imply, however, that TOP was always explicitly under discussion in these studies. Mostly the temporal perception was inherent to the task set.

The Digit Span (DS) of the Wechsler Intelligence Scale for Children (WISC) illustrates this: S hears a number of digits and is asked to reproduce them in the sequence of presentation. Belmont & Birch (1966) made an extensive study of the WISC-profiles of 150 reading-disturbed children and 50 normal readers. This study showed that of the verbal subtests the DS was one of the discriminators between normal and disturbed. That reading-disturbed Ss score lower on this subtest than normal readers do, is also shown by other sources: Belmont & Birch mention some of them. We may add the recent studies of Lyle & Goyen (1969) and of Kinsbourne & Warrington (1966).

Digits are verbal stimuli, unlike the elements of a tapped-out rhythmic pattern. These elements, however, can be codified verbally: .–. may be rendered as 'short long short'.

20

If one has patterns labelled in this way, reading-disturbed *S*s appear to have more difficulty in performing this than normal readers. This was shown by Blank & Bridger (1966) and later by Blank, Weider & Bridger (1968) by means of tests in which children of 9 to 10 and of 6 to 7 years old respectively participated.

An extensive and thorough investigation of the VI-type was recently conducted by Senf (1969). He examined the memory for bisensory stimuli with normal and learning-disturbed boys. *S*s varied in age from about 9 to 13. Several experiments were carried out, the second of which is particularly relevant. Pairs of digits were presented to *S*, of each pair one digit visually and one digit auditorily; for instance V1/A2, V3/A4 and V5/A6, in which V stands for visual and A for auditory. Some *S*s had to reproduce the digits *by pairs* (1, 2, 3, 4, 5, 6), others *by modality* (1, 3, 5, 2, 4, 6), in both cases in the sequence of presentation.

Learning-disturbed children appear to make far more mistakes than normal children. This holds good especially when reproduction in pairs is asked for. In that case the differences between the groups increase with age. With reproduction by modality, on the other hand, the differences between the groups are greatest at younger ages.

Senf carried out a third experiment, in which meaningful figures were used instead of digits. The results were much the same as those of the second experiment.

Another important conclusion Senf could come to was that learning-disturbed and normal children do not differ significantly with regard to the total number of digits that were reproduced correctly (leaving sequence out of consideration). From this it is evident that the perception and retention of the *sequence* of the digits and not so much the retention of the digits themselves discriminates between normal and disturbed children. 'This distinction is very important in that reading skills are heavily dependent on correct sequential ordering of events' (p. 27).

In summary we can say that the studies of the VI-type as opposed to those of the NI-type lead unanimously to the conclusion that TOP is positively related to reading ability.

4. NONVERBAL AND VERBAL EXPLICATION (NE & VE) STUDIES

Introduction. It is characteristic of explication studies that the serial location of the items in a series of items is explicitly asked for. The items can be of a verbal and a nonverbal nature, and on the analogy of this we may speak of verbal and nonverbal explication studies.

There is little research of the NE-type available, and that is the reason why the discussion of studies of this and of the VE-type are combined here.

Temporal order perception in relation to reading ability has been subject of research in our laboratory for several years. In most of these studies *S*s were required to explicate TOP.

Background studies. The motive of our programme was a series of investigations by Birch and associates in New York. This group investigates auditory-visual integration by means of a test that has become known as the BB-test named after its designers Birch & Belmont (1964, 1965). A rhythmic pattern is presented to *S* who is asked to look up the pattern he heard on a card with a number of alternatives. So *S* has to match something he hears with something he sees. But there is more. The stimuli *S* hears are ordered in time and the stimuli he sees are ordered in space. Thus what matters in the BB-test is the matching of auditory-temporal with visual-spatial configurations.

A predecessor of the BB-test had been constructed by Borel-Maisonny and described in the above-mentioned article by Stamback (1951). E shows *S* a card with a number of rhythmic patterns. All patterns have an equal number of elements which, however, are grouped in various ways. E taps out one of the patterns and asks *S* to indicate on the card which pattern was presented. We see that this test and the BB-test are much alike. Besides, the results obtained by Stamback and the Birch-group are in the same line: reading-disturbed children make far more mistakes in matching than normal children.

The scores of the BB-test discriminate not only between normal and reading-disturbed children, they also appear to correlate significantly with reading ability within these groups (Lovell & Gorton, 1968; Kahn & Birch, 1968).

It is obvious that the matching of auditory-temporal with visual-spatial patterns represents a complex factor, in which, among other things, a temporal moment is to be distinguished. The temporal pattern that E taps out has to be perceived and retained by *S*. It is conceivable that reading-disturbed children find this very difficult and that their comparatively bad results with the BB-test are partly due to this.

This hypothesis was tested by Blank, Weider & Bridger (1968). The results of their investigation have already been mentioned: reading-disturbed children appear to have no difficulty in imitating the rhythmic patterns nonverbally (NI-task), but they do have difficulty in imitating them verbally (VI-task).

Personal NE- and VE-studies. The research at our laboratory runs parallel to that of the Blank-group, but yet differs in method from it on two points.

Instead of tapped-out patterns we use as stimuli letters, digits, meaningful and meaningless figures, and the like. They can be divided into three categories, namely verbal stimuli (letters, digits), verbally codifiable stimuli (meaningful figures) and nonverbal stimuli (meaningless figures). The variability is an advantage of this kind of stimulus-material; with tapped-out patterns one mostly does not get beyond the distinction short-long (*. vs. –*).

A second characteristic of our investigations is that we asked explicitly for the serial locations of the items, mostly with the help of a reconstruction method. When referring to the serial locations of verbal stimuli (letters, digits) or verbally codifiable stimuli (meaningful figures) one may speak of an investigation of the VE-type. If experiments are made with nonverbal stimuli such as meaningless figures, one is dealing with investigations of the NE-type. In NE-research it is natural to use a reconstruction method: meaningless figures have no label and can therefore not be reproduced vocally. During the reconstruction the figures presented before are being recognized. This has the advantage that *S* will not have to retain the items themselves but only their sequence of presentation. By asking explicitly for the serial locations of the items the importance of the sequence factor is specially emphasized in the set-up.

In our first investigation (Bakker, 1967) boys from a school for learning-disturbed children participated. The reading ability of these children is below the national standard. The children were divided into below-average (BA) and above-average (AA) readers, and for this division the median of the reading ability scores served as the cut-off point.

The stimuli presented to *S*s in temporal succession were letters and digits, meaningful figures and meaningless figures. The four items of each series were presented one by one with the help of a tachistoscope. After presentation of a series a card was handed out, on which the pictures that had just been seen were represented (reconstruction method).

S had to indicate which item was shown first and which one came next, and so on. So the sequence of each item in the series was explicitly asked for. The BA-readers appeared to make significantly more errors than the AA-readers in the perception and retention of series of letters, digits and meaningful figures, but just as many mistakes with regard to series of meaningless figures. A difference between letters, digits and meaningful figures on the one hand and meaningless figures on the other, is that while the former items are either verbal or verbally codifiable in nature, neither can be said of meaningless figures.

The interpretation of these results can be defined as follows: TOP is related to the learning-to-read process, but only if in the perception and retention of the temporal sequences a verbal medium is operant. If no verbal medium is available, as is the case with the meaningless figures, the two groups of readers cannot be distinguished.

A second investigation was carried out with normal children of 7 and 10 years old (Groenendaal & Bakker, 1971). The children were again divided into BA- and AA-readers. This time only series of meaningful figures and series of meaningless figures were presented. The procedure, however, was similar to that of the first investigation. From this study, too, it appeared that the perception and retention of series of meaningful figures correlate in general with reading ability, but the perception and retention of meaningless figures do not.

A third investigation was again carried out with boys of a school for learning difficulties (Muller & Bakker, 1968). Here visual stimuli were presented two at a time in temporal succession. Two coloured flashes were shown with a stimulus duration of 100 Msec. and an interval of 75 Msec. After each presentation one of the two colours was mentioned and S had to say whether this colour was shown first or last. A few differences with the two preceding studies can be noted. In these studies the stimulus duration of each item was approximately 2 sec., whereas the interval between two items was of more or less the same duration. In the investigation of Muller & Bakker these values were considerably lower. This was done intentionally in order to link up in procedure with studies on the relations between TOP and defects in spoken language, studies which will be discussed later. For in these investigations relatively short stimulus durations and intervals were used. A second difference with the studies that were discussed earlier is that in the investigation of Muller *et al.* no reconstruction method was used.

In spite of these differences the results were again as was to be expected: AA-readers retained correctly 71% of the series, BA-readers only 58%, a statistically significant difference.

Finally, an investigation with the youngest children of a primary school (Fossen, 1969). These first-formers received series of black-and-white and series of coloured letters (the coloured letters were used with a view to a question that is not under discussion here). Stimulus duration and time of interval were kept as constant as possible at 1 sec. Ss had to retain the presentation order of the letters. Here, too, AA-readers appeared to score considerably higher than BA-readers. TOP correlated $+.63$ with reading ability. So also at an early age does TOP appear to be related to normal reading ability. As a peculiarity may be mentioned the fact that girls were

24

inclined to retain the black-and-white series better than boys.

The conclusion that can be arrived at on the ground of these four studies is that TOP, made operational as verbal explication of temporal series, is related to the normal and the disturbed learning-to-read process.

In fact reading ability is usually measured by psychometric tests. The score of the test often depends on the number of errors made. This number, however, does not say anything about the nature of the mistakes.

Reading- and writing-errors can be classified in many different ways (Van der Wissel, 1963; Bakker, 1965). A kind of error rather frequently observed is that of anti- and retrocipations: 'stale' is read instead of 'slate' and 'brain' instead of 'by train'. For us it was an interesting question whether children with a relatively low score on a temporal ordering task make comparatively many of these anti- and retrocipation errors. An investigation into this was found to confirm the expectations (Leene & Bakker, 1969). In reading, relatively poor temporal order perceivers (classified on the ground of a task in which series of meaningful figures and digits were presented) made as many as four times more anti- and retrocipation errors than good temporal order perceivers did.

5. TOP AND WRITTEN LANGUAGE: CONCLUSIONS AND DISCUSSION

In the discussion of his results Senf (1969) states that '... the LDC's (Learning Disturbed Children) failures were generally specific to the ordering of stimuli, not to their accuracy of recall' and that 'Further study needs to address itself to the generality and nature of this deficit' (p. 26–27).

More about the nature of the deficit Senf speaks of can probably be said at this point, referring to said studies dealing with the relations between TOP and reading ability. Senf used digits and meaningful figures in his experiments, i.e. verbal or verbally codifiable material. The same happened in the investigations by Bakker and associates. But in their studies meaningless figures were used as well, i.e. material that is not verbally codifiable. Two conclusions seem justified. First that our results are entirely in line with those of Senf. Secondly that Senf's speaking of failures in the ordering of stimuli with reading-disturbed children is too generally stated: the failures do not apply to all stimuli, but only to those which are verbal in nature or verbally codifiable.

This restriction seems necessary in view of the results which were obtained by the Blank-group with the nonverbal imitation of rhythmic patterns and by us with the perception and retention of meaningless figures. For in these conditions normal and reading-disturbed children do not appear to be different.

25

Recapitulating, it can be stated that TOP, if made operational either in a verbally-imitating way or in a verbally-explicating way, appears to be related to reading ability. In NI- and NE-studies, on the other hand, no clear TOP-reading relations were found.

Furthermore the contrast between imitation and explication appears not to be decisive for either the existence or non-existence of a TOP-reading relation. Not unrelated to this will be the common characteristic of imitation and explication, viz. that both refer to the reproduction of temporal patterns.

The studies mentioned provide some evidence that TOP conditions reading ability and not the other way round. For in a number of experiments (DeHirsch, Jansky & Langford, 1966; Blank, Weider & Bridger, 1968; Leene & Bakker, 1969; Fossen, 1969) young children participated who had received no or hardly any education in reading. Nevertheless a TOP-reading relation was found, and that is why Blank *et al.* could conclude that 'deficiencies in verbalization of complex material are present at the onset of reading retardation and may be responsible for, rather than be a result of, reading difficulties' (p. 833).

So a TOP-reading relation at an early age exists. How this relation develops with increasing age has not become quite clear. It is certain that TOP at a later age discriminates between normal and reading-disturbed (Belmont & Birch, 1966; Senf, 1969) and correlates with the reading ability of disturbed children (Bakker, 1967; Muller & Bakker, 1968). But whether this correlation applies to the reading ability of older normal children is doubtful. With normal children Groenendaal & Bakker (1971) found a smaller correlation at the age of 10 than at the age of 7.

From these data one might conclude that the TOP-reading relation does not depend on age but on the reading ability level. This level is high with normal children of an older age, but comparatively low with disturbed children of the same age. Thus, one might argue, the relation is (still) present in disturbed children of an older age, but not (any more) in normal children of an older age.

This line of thought leads to the question how TOP itself develops with age. Little more can be said here about this problem, except that there appears to be a development in normal children, but hardly any in disturbed children (Stamback, 1951). This datum is in itself of course interesting enough. For the fact that TOP does not develop in reading-disturbed children is probably one of the causes of their handicap in reading.

Only one study points out sex-differences with regard to the TOP-reading relation. DeHirsch, Jansky & Langford (1966) found a stronger relation in girls than in boys. In this context it should be noted, however,

26

that this study dealt with comparatively young children (5 to 8 years old).

On the ground of the investigations discussed one must draw the conclusion that a TOP-reading relation exists, but that this statement is limited in its generality. The limitation is, among other things, connected with the nature (verbal *vs.* nonverbal) of the temporal order.

6. TOP AND SPOKEN LANGUAGE

The perception and retention of temporal order appears to be related to spoken language no less than to written language.

Explication studies. Some years ago Hirsh (1959) and Hirsh & Sherrick (1961) examined the perception of temporal order in adults as follows. Two stimuli (2 different tones, 2 different flashes of light, etc.) were presented to S in rapid succession. S had to indicate which of the stimuli was presented first or last. It appeared that Ss needed an interval of at least 20 Msec. in order to be able to determine the sequence. This interval did not vary with the nature of the stimuli so that it could be suggested that central processes were at the root of the perception of temporal order.

A few years later Efron (1963a) applied a similar method for a comparative examination of aphasic and non-aphasic adults. Aphasic patients appeared to require a much longer interstimulus interval than the non-aphasics in order to be able to determine the correct temporal order. Lowe & Campbell (1965) found a similar difference between aphasoid and normal children.

Malone (1967), however, found no relation between the perception of temporal order and the ability to identify words presented at varying rates. In this respect it should be noted that this investigator did not wholly follow the procedure of Hirsh. Hirsh had his Ss write down which tone, the high tone or the low one, they had heard first. In Malone's investigation the Ss had to press one of two buttons each time in order to indicate whether the high tone or the low one was presented first. This is a slight difference, but perhaps important. In examinations of Hirsh's type the responses are to be given verbally, but not so with Malone. The procedure followed by Hirsh is clearly of the VE-type, whereas there is no certainty about Malone's procedure. It is very well possible that during Malone's investigation a sequence-place (tone-button) association developed with the Ss, in which verbalization of the tones hardly played a part.

If this is correct, then the fact that Efron could determine a TOP-language relation but Malone could not is to be explained by the verbal codification of stimuli in the former study and the absence of such codification in the latter study.

Imitation studies. While in the studies by Hirsh, Efron, and others the serial location of the items was to be explicated, there are also investigations in which temporal series were reproduced through imitation.

Stark (1967) presented the Auditory-Vocal Sequencing subtest of the ITPA-battery to aphasic children. In this test *S* has to repeat a series of numbers pronounced by E in correct order. The children appeared to be retarded by more than two years compared with the norm for their age. With a nonverbal imitation test, the Knox Cube Tapping Test, the children also appeared to be retarded, though much less. The distinction verbal-nonverbal may be a factor in this difference in results.

Monsees (1968) asked a number of children with expressive language difficulties to repeat in correct order a series of phonemes that make up an existing or a nonsense word. The results were compared with those of normal children. The scores of the disturbed children were clearly lower than those of the normal children.

Comparing the various studies of the relations between TOP and spoken language, one notices that there is a relationship in method as well as in result with the studies on the relations between TOP and written language. In both cases the relation appears to be substantial. But this was only the case when a verbal mediation process played an essential part in the temporal perception.

7. SOME OTHER TOP STUDIES

Two other studies are worth mentioning. They are relevant because of their method of investigation and aim. The studies in question were concerned not only with the perception of temporal order in normal children but also with the relation between TOP and intelligence.

In an investigation of factors related to the acquisition of verbal language by Furth & Youniss (1967) seven- and ten-year-old children from a normal primary school took part. The seven-year-olds as well as the ten-year-olds were divided into a group with above-average IQs (AA-group) and one with below-average IQs (BA-group). One of the tasks was the reproduction of the order in which a number of nonsense figures was shown. In these tasks a reconstruction method was used: after successive presentation of the figures they were, simultaneously, shown once again

28

and *S* had to indicate what had been the sequence of presentation. The procedure followed is of the NE-type and appears to be almost similar to the one usually followed in our laboratory. The older children obtained better results than the younger ones and the AA-group scored better than the BA-group.

The relation between intelligence and the perception of series of nonsense figures is interesting. With a view to this result the data of an investigation mentioned before (Bakker, 1967) were studied in connection with the IQs of the children. It appeared that the children of our sample with an above-average IQ retained the series of nonsense figures better than the children with a below-average IQ. This result agrees with the one obtained by Furth & Youniss. The perception and retention of series of nonsense figures is evidently not related to reading ability but to IQ. The children of our sample came from a school where the WISC is generally used for determining the IQ. This test has a verbal and a performal part. The common variance of IQ and memory for series of nonsense figures can be explained by the nonverbal character of these figures on the one hand and by the performal part of the WISC on the other. Unfortunately, Furth & Youniss do not mention the intelligence test used by them.

Ross & Youniss (1969) studied the memory for temporal order in children of 6 and 10 years old. Both series of meaningful figures and series of meaningless figures were presented. Memory for temporal order was found to be clearly related to age. The scores on meaningless figures were lower than those on meaningful figures. Interesting, too, is that six-year-old children order less spontaneously than ten-year-old children. This holds good for meaningful as well as meaningless figures. Evidently ordering becomes more and more a strategy at a later age.

8. SUMMARY AND PREFACE

A number of studies on the relations between language behaviour and the perception of temporal order have now been reviewed. The temporal order concept does not appear to get attention explicitly in all cases and where it does there is a difference in the operational definition of this time concept.

The perception of temporal order appears in the literature in four ways. TOP is taken as a. verbally-imitating (VI-type), b. nonverbally-imitating (NI-type), c. verbally-explicating (VE-type) or d. nonverbally-explicating (NE-type). In these forms TOP was studied in relation to written language, spoken language and some other variables.

Under certain conditions TOP appears to be related to both written language (reading) and spoken language (speech). One may state, therefore, that there is a TOP-language relation. This relation seems, however, only then present when TOP is taken as verbally-imitating or verbally-explicating. In other words, verbal-temporal perception is related to language behaviour, whereas nonverbal-temporal perception is not or less related to it.

This is not really surprising. Written and spoken language are verbal as well as temporal processes. These processes are simulated more by verbally-imitating and verbally-explicating procedures than by their non-verbal counterparts.

At all ages investigated, i.e. from 5 to 15 years old, a TOP-reading relation was found, both in normal and in reading- (learning-) disturbed children. The relation is recognizable as a quantity (number of errors in reading) and as a quality (nature of errors).

TOP itself improves with age, but does so slower in reading-disturbed children than in normal ones.

It is possible that girls score better in TOP than boys, at least so at younger ages; in them the TOP-reading relation seems also stronger than in boys.

The following chapters describe a number of extensive investigations in which especially the relations between TOP on the one hand and reading ability, age and sex on the other are further examined. TOP will be made operational exclusively in a verbally-explicating way.

This on account of the now well-founded opinion that optimal TOP-relations may be expected with this procedure.

The following hypotheses will be tested. They proceed from the results of the studies that have been reviewed so far.

TOP correlates:

I.   positively with age in normal children,
II. positively with age in reading- (learning-) disturbed children,
III. positively with age to a greater extent in normal children than in reading-disturbed ones,
IV. positively with the reading ability of normal children,
V.   positively with the reading ability of reading-disturbed children.

TOP differentiates:

VI. at all ages investigated between normal and reading-disturbed children,

VII. at younger ages between boys and girls.

Secondary problems will naturally also come up for discussion. Whenever they are dealt with, explanatory notes will be given.

III. Investigations into temporal order perception: Pre-school and primary school children

1. INTRODUCTION

This investigation in which normal children between 5 and 9 years old took part, aimed at testing the hypotheses I, IV and VII (Ch. II. 8) concerning the relations between TOP on the one hand and age, reading ability and sex on the other. In the preceding chapter the backgrounds of these hypotheses have been described.

From a number of investigations (Stamback, 1951; Groenendaal & Bakker, 1971; Senf, 1969) it appeared that older children score better in TOP than younger ones. Since more than two groups of different ages have been involved in the present investigation it is possible to check what the nature of the TOP-age relation is. Moreover, possible interactions of age with other main variables can be studied.

Investigations by Stamback (1951), DeHirsch, Jansky & Langford (1966), Blank, Weider & Bridger (1968), Fossen (1969) and Groenendaal & Bakker (1971) have proved that TOP correlates positively with reading ability also at younger ages.

It is generally known that more boys than girls are liable to reading difficulties (Eisenberg, 1966). This knowledge has induced some people to suppose that girls of 4 to 7 years old perform better than boys with regard to factors connected with the learning-to-read process. Such differences in sex were found by Sapir (1966) and Keogh & Smith (1967) among others. Fossen (1969) demonstrated that first grade boys score lower in TOP than first grade girls.

2. METHOD

Subjects. 412 children from nursery-schools participated in the investigation (208 boys and 204 girls). These infants formed a representative sample of the Dutch nursery-school children of that age (M = 6.3).

32

Material and procedure. Two tests were presented to the children, called TOVV (temporal ordering visual-visual) and TOAV (temporal ordering auditory-visual), respectively. Both tests were concerned with the perception and retention of the place of each item in a series of items presented in temporal succession.

With TOVV presentation was visual. The items were pictures of ordinary objects, represented on separate small cards (Fig. 2). The pictures were shown to *S* one by one. Stimulus duration and time of interval were kept as constant as possible (about two sec. each). After presentation of a series the pictures that had been shown were all at the same time presented to *S*. *S* subsequently had to indicate which picture E had shown first, which second etc. There were three series of 3, five series of 4 and two series of 5 pictures. The shortest series were started with. There was a set instruction. Series plus instruction had been tried out before at a nursery-school (not belonging to the sample). At the beginning of the session a test-trial was given in order to be sure that the task was understood.

Fig. 2.   Pictures of TOVV and TOAV

*S*s were not allowed to name the pictures aloud. When 3 successive trials were wrong, there was no further continuation. The trials were scored either correct (all pictures of the series put in correct order) or wrong (one or more pictures in the wrong place). As there were 10 series a maximum of 10 points could be scored.

With TOAV presentation was auditory. The items were the same as with TOVV. But the pictures were now named aloud by E. Having called out a series E again laid down the card with all pictures mentioned in front of *S*. *S* had to indicate which picture E had mentioned first and which came next. In all, two series of 2, four of 3, five of 4 and one series of 5 pictures were presented. So *S* could score 12 points at most. Preliminary testing, instruction and scoring were just as with TOVV.

TOVV and TOAV are tasks of the VE-type. In view of the age of the children (5- and 6-year-olds from nursery-schools) it was decided that meaningful pictures (verbally codifiable material) and no letters (verbal material) would be used for the composition of the series. TOAV is unlike TOVV an intermodal matching task (auditory-visual) and shows as such similarities with the BB-test (Birch & Belmont, 1964a, 1965).

In addition to TOVV and TOAV an intelligence test was taken (Drenth, Petrie & Bleichrodt, 1968). TOAV was repeated with the same children after one and two years, i.e. in the first and second form of the primary school. At the same ages (M = 7.3 and M = 8.3) reading ability scores were determined as well (Wiegersma, 1958).

3. RESULTS

TOVV in relation to age and sex. The results were analysed in a 2 × 2 design with age and sex as variables. The children were divided into two age groups for which the median served as the cut-off point. The below-

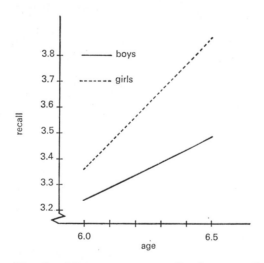

Fig. 3. Mean correct recall of temporal sequences (TOVV) by sex and age

34

average group (BA) had an average age of 6.0 years and the above-average group (AA) one of 6.5 years.

The results are rendered graphically in Fig. 3. Only the age factor appeared to be significant ($F = 5.14$; $df = 1,408$; $p < .025$). Girls are inclined to score better than boys, especially at the age of 6.5. The sex difference, however, was not significant ($F = 2.40$; $df = 1,408$; $p > .10$), no more than the sex × age interaction ($F = .34$; $df = 1,408$; $p > .25$).

TOAV in relation to age and sex (cross sectional study). As with TOVV results were analysed in a 2 × 2 design with sex and age as variables.

All factors appeared to be significant (age: $F = 13.62$; $df = 1,408$; $p < .001$; sex: $F = 10.22$; $df = 1,408$; $p < .005$ and age × sex: $F = 5.91$; $df = 1,408$; $p < .025$). As with TOVV the sex and age differences cannot be explained by IQ differences between groups (Mean IQs: younger boys = 100.7, younger girls = 99.6, older boys = 99.0, older girls = 97.9).

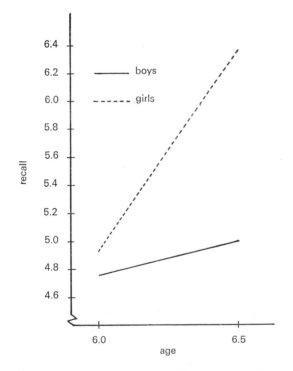

Fig. 4. *Mean correct recall of temporal sequences (TOAV) by sex and age*

The results are shown in Fig. 4. It is clear that girls improve more with age than boys and that especially the results of the older girls are better than those of the older boys.

TOAV in relation to age and sex (longitudinal study). The results were analysed in a 2 × 3 design with sex and age (repeated measures at ages of 6.3, 7.3, and 8.3) as variables.

The two main factors appeared to be significant (sex: $F = 8.32$; $df = 1,354$; $p < .005$ and age: $F = 559.64$; $df = 2,708$; $p = <.005$), the sex × age interaction was not significant ($F = .65$; $df = 2,708$; $p > .25$). The results are given in Fig. 5.

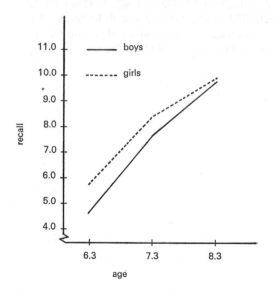

Fig. 5.   *Mean correct recall of temporal sequences (TOAV) by sex and age (longitudinal)*

The differences between girls and boys become smaller with increasing age. Further analysis (Winer, 1962) yields significant sex differences at ages 6 and 7 (6 years old: $F = 10.00$; $df = 1,1062$; $p < .005$ and 7 years old: $F = 5.20$; $df = 1,1062$; $p < .025$), but not at the age of 8 ($F = 1.20$; $df = 1,1062$; $p > .25$).

TOVV and TOAV in relation to reading ability. The results of a correlation analysis are found in Table 1.

36

Table 1. Correlations (Product-Moment Coefficients) between Reading ability, TOVV, TOAV, and IQ at different ages

	1	2	3	4	5	6	7
1 TOVV-at the age of 6		.38[1]	.22	.15	.28	.30	.32
2 TOAV-at the age of 6			.46	.26	.38	.38	.38
3 TOAV-at the age of 7				.33	.39	.38	.39
4 TOAV-at the age of 8					.27	.32	.42
5 IQ -at the age of 6						.42	.47
6 Reading ability-at the age of 7							.80
7 Reading ability-at the age of 8							

R 6.12 = .42 (F^2 = 37.81; df = 2,353; p <.005)
R 7.12 = .43 (F = 40.03; df = 2,353; p <.005)
r 16.5 = .21 (t = 4.20; df = 353; p <.0005)
r 17.5 = .23 (t = 4.60; df = 353; p <.0005)
r 26.5 = .27 (t = 5.40; df = 353; p <.0005)
r 27.5 = .24 (t = 4.80; df = 353; p <.0005)

All r- and R-values are positive.
1. All r-values of the matrix are significant at 1% level.
2. Hays, 1963.

TOAV correlates with reading ability to a higher extent than TOVV does. Multiple correlation of TOVV and TOAV with reading is about as high as the correlation between IQ and reading. The correlation of TOVV and TOAV with reading ability is smaller when the IQ-effect is eliminated. The partial correlation coefficients are very significant, however. One may conclude, therefore, that TOP in pre-school and primary school children is related to reading ability. This is in conformity with the hypothesis.

4. SUMMARY AND DISCUSSION

The perception and retention of temporal order is clearly related to age (Hypothesis I).Even in less than six months the values of the TOVV- and TOAV-scores (Figs. 3 and 4) increase significantly.

During a period of two years (6 to 7) the scores on TOAV improve strongly (Fig. 5); after these ages the increase is not quite so large.

Girls generally score better in TOP than boys at the ages of 6 and 7 (Hypothesis VII). This is most obvious with TOAV. A year later the boys have caught up with the girls. So on entering the primary-school girls seem in this respect to be better equipped than boys.

This remark makes sense only if TOP is causally related to the learning-to-read process.

From the significant correlations between TOVV/TOAV and reading ability it appeared that there is a relation between TOP and reading (Hypothesis IV). A correlation between A and B, however, does not imply that a change in A produces a change in B, or in other words, that there is a dependence relation between these variables (Fokkema, 1967). Inherent to the causal relation is the temporal moment: A can only bring about a change in B if A precedes B (Blalock, 1964; De Wit & Bakker, 1971).

A temporal moment is clearly present in our investigation. TOVV and TOAV, taken at a time when Ss cannot yet read, correlate with reading ability at a *later* age. On the ground of this temporal relation it can be said that TOP-scores do certainly not depend on reading. The opposite, viz. reading ability is to a certain extent directly or indirectly determined by the capacity of temporal ordering, is more probable.

A connection found between variables can be interesting in etiological as well as predictive respect. TOVV and TOAV together, taken at the nursery-school, explain about 18% of the variance in the reading ability scores obtained one or two years later. The intelligence test accounts for about a similar part of the variance. Keogh & Smith (1967) found that the Bender-Gestalt Test (taken at nursery-school age) explains about the same percentage of variance in reading-scores (obtained in the 3rd and 6th forms of elementary schools) as TOVV and TOAV. The usefulness of TOVV and TOAV as means of prediction seems to be limited in view of the rather low amount of explained variance in the reading scores. The same may be said of the Bender Test.

TOAV appears to be more strongly related to sex and reading ability than TOVV. TOAV is a more complex task than TOVV. With TOAV not only temporal ordering is required but auditory-visual integration as well; stimuli that are heard are to be matched with stimuli that are seen. Apart from temporal ordering, between modality matching is also an aspect of the actual reading and writing process. Reading consequently seems to be simulated more by TOAV than by TOVV, on the ground of which the higher correlations between TOAV and reading ability can be explained.

IV. Investigations into temporal order perception: Relations to age and sex in normal and learning-disturbed children

1. INTRODUCTION

The investigation now up for discussion was carried out with normal boys and girls between the ages of 7 and 11 and with reading-disturbed boys between the ages of 9 and 13. In this chapter the relations between TOP on the one hand, and age and sex on the other will be discussed; the hypotheses I, II, III and VII (Ch. II. 8) will be tested.

The normal and reading-disturbed children were not, as were the nursery-school children of the preceding investigation, presented with series of figures but series of letters in temporal succession. The reason for this is simply that 7- to 13-year-old children know the letters whereas children of a nursery-school generally do not. By using letters instead of figures the actual learning-to-read process is simulated better.

The letters were presented under three sensory conditions: visual, haptic and auditory. This was done in order to determine to what extent TOP depends on the sensory input. Hirsh & Sherrick (1961) found a complete independence of the two factors: in order to be able to determine the sequence of two visual stimuli one generally needs an interstimulus interval of at least 20 Msec.; a similar interval is needed with auditory and tactile stimuli. This mutual independence of TOP and input leads them to the conclusion that TOP is a central process.

Rosenbusch & Gardner (1968), on the other hand, came to an entirely different conclusion. They presented to their Ss, normal children of 5 to 13 years old, visual and auditory rhythmic patterns. These patterns had to be reproduced by S by means of a telegraph key. At all ages more errors were made with a visual input than with an auditory one. Conclusion of the authors (p. 1274): 'It is clear that the processing of rhythmic information by the child is a function of the sensory modality in which the information is presented'.

The contradictory conclusions of the two investigations are no doubt connected with differences in method and procedure. Referring to a distinction made earlier one may state that the task of Rosenbusch *et al.* was nonverbally-imitating (NI-type) in nature and the one of Hirsh *et al.* explicating with verbal codification of the stimuli (VE-type). In other words, in the task of Hirsh & Sherrick a distinct verbal moment is found, whereas this is at the least doubtful in the task given by Rosenbusch & Gardner. The difference in conclusion with regard to the relation between TOP and sensory input is perhaps, among other things, due to this difference in verbal participation. It is of course also important to point out that Hirsh & Sherrick involved adults in their investigation, whereas Rosenbusch & Gardner worked with children.

In the present study temporal series of letters were presented in a visual, tactile-kinaesthetic (haptic) and auditory way. The fact that letters were presented is probably more important than the difference in sensory input. For the verbal-symbolic character of a letter may be considered to be a 'supra-modal feature' (Von Wright, 1969) which is so pregnant that the modal specificity of the stimulus will play no or at least a non-perceptible part in the temporal ordering process.

We expect therefore that the sensory input will effect no systematic variance in the results. This prediction is based on the assumption that the verbal-symbolic aspect of the material really plays the major part in the processing of the temporal series.

2. METHOD

Subjects. In the investigation 175 children participated, 100 normal boys and girls of an elementary school (Mean IQ = 108.1) and 75 learning-disturbed boys of two schools for learning and educational difficulties (Mean IQ = 96.4).

The normal children varied in age from 7 to 11 years, 10 boys and 10 girls at each age level, at random selected from their classes. The learning-disturbed boys varied in age from 9 to 13 years, 15 Ss at each age level.

Material and procedure. In all, 48 series of 3 letters were presented: 16 series visually, 16 haptically and 16 auditorily (condition-sequence counterbalanced). The letters were presented in temporal succession. The presentation time of a letter as well as the interval between two letters was about 2 sec. under the visual and auditory condition.

After each series 2 of 3 letters were presented again visually, haptically or auditorily and S had to indicate whether he had perceived these two letters first, second or last. This reconstruction method was maintained with a view to the unity of procedure in respect of the other experiments (Ch. III).

An answer was correct or wrong so that a maximum of 16 points could be scored per sensory input.

Under visual and haptic conditions letters that were cut into a square piece of wood were used. For the auditory condition the series were recorded on a tape. Under the haptic condition the Ss were blindfolded. They were allowed to touch the letters with both hands. When S thought he had explored a letter well enough, he indicated this by putting the letter aside.

The instruction was the same for every one. From test-trials it was concluded whether S had understood the task. S was not allowed to name the letters aloud.

For the composition of the series the following letters were used: C, D, G, K, V, X, Z.

3. RESULTS

TOP in normal children. The results were analysed in a 5 (age) × 2 (sex) × 3 (sensory mode) design with repeated measures on the last factor.

All main factors appeared to be significant: age ($F = 34.42$; $df = 4,90$; $p < .005$), sex ($F = 6.86$; $df = 1,90$; $p < .025$) and sensory mode ($F = 20.03$; $df = 2,180$; $p < .001$). One interaction was significant: age × sex ($F = 3.25$; $df = 4,90$; $p < .025$).

The results are given graphically in Fig. 6. The age × sex interaction is evidently to be interpreted in such a way that 7- and 8-year-old girls give better performances than boys, but not any more so at later ages. Considering the absence of a significant age × sex × mode interaction ($F = .59$; $df = 8,180$; $p > .10$) this evidently applies to each of the input conditions.

The nature of the age × sex interaction is strikingly illustrated by Fig. 7 in which the results are presented across sensory modes.

With a visual and auditory input better results are obtained than with a haptic one. This apparently applies to boys and girls of all ages, considering the fact that neither the sex × mode interaction ($F = 1.46$; $df = 2,180$; $p > .10$), nor the age × mode interaction ($F = 1.17$; $df = = 8,180$; $p > .10$) are significant. Fig. 8 in which the performances of boys and girls are pooled, clearly shows the differences in results with a visual and auditory input on the one hand and with a haptic one on the other. The

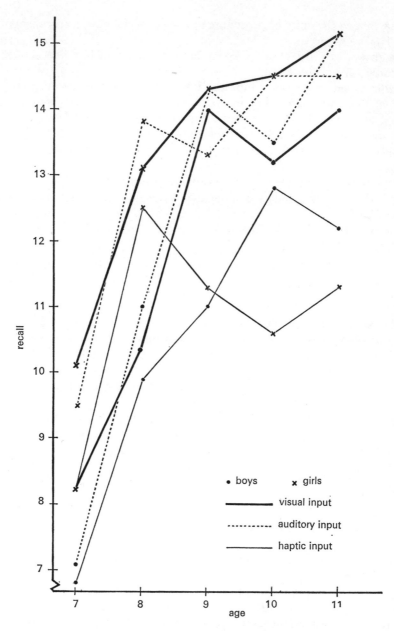

Fig. 6. Mean correct recall of temporal sequences by sensory modality for normal boys and normal girls of different age

42

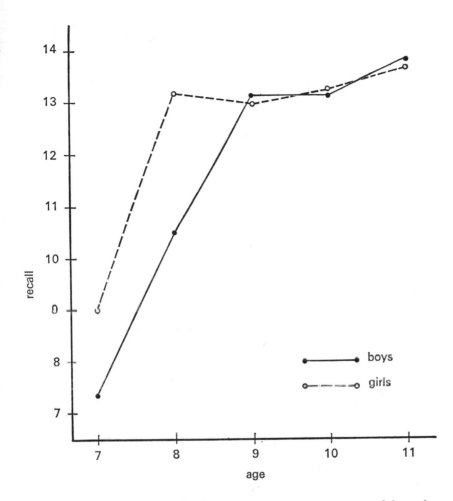

*Fig. 7. Mean correct recall of temporal sequences across modalities by
sex and age for normal children*

differences become striking after the age of eight, a result that is illustrated
by a strong levelling-off of the haptic curve after this age.

TOP in learning-disturbed boys. The results were analysed in a 5 (age) ×
× 3 (sensory mode) design with repeated measures on the last factor. Both
main factors (age: $F = 10.20$; $df = 4,70$; $p < .001$ and mode: $F = 19.35$;
$df = 2,140$; $p < .001$) appeared to be significant, but not their interaction

43

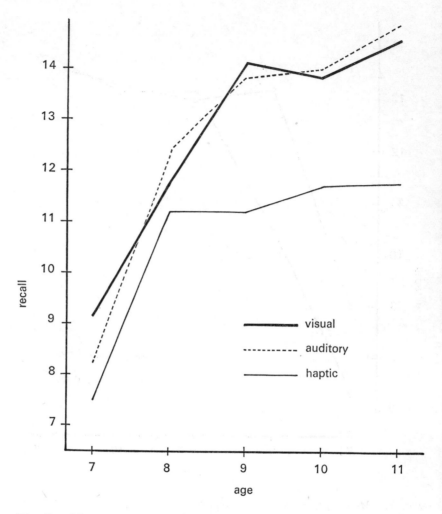

Fig. 8. Mean correct recall of temporal sequences across sexes by modality and age for normal children

($F = 1.21$; $df = 8,140$; $p > .10$). Fig. 9 shows the results graphically. The significant variance which is caused by the sensory input is in Fig. 9 found to be reflected in the difference between the visual and auditory curves on the one hand and the haptic curve on the other.

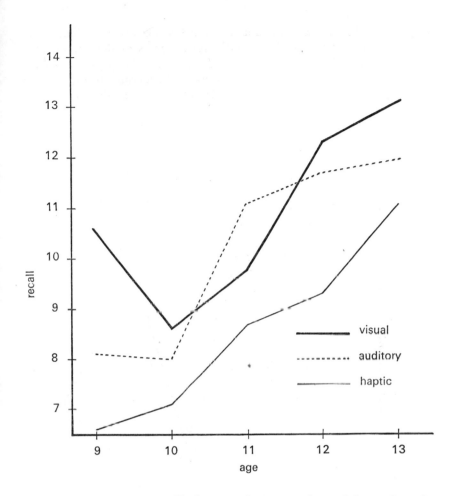

Fig. 9. Mean correct recall of temporal sequences by modality and age for learning-disturbed boys

4. ADDITIONAL RESULTS

Figures 8 and 9 clearly show that the TOP-scores are higher with a visual and auditory input than with a haptic one. With presentation to each of the two telereceptors performances hardly differ.

For further investigation of the relation between input-channel and TOP the haptic scores were subtracted from the average visual and auditory scores. These intra-individual difference scores are according to age and sex rendered in Fig. 10. The difference scores of the normal boys ($t = 2.63$; $df = 49$; $p < .025$, two-tailed), and the normal girls ($t = 4.94$; $df = 49$; $p < .01$, two-tailed), as well as of the learning-disturbed boys ($t = 3.30$; $df = 74$; $p < .01$, two-tailed), differ significantly from zero.

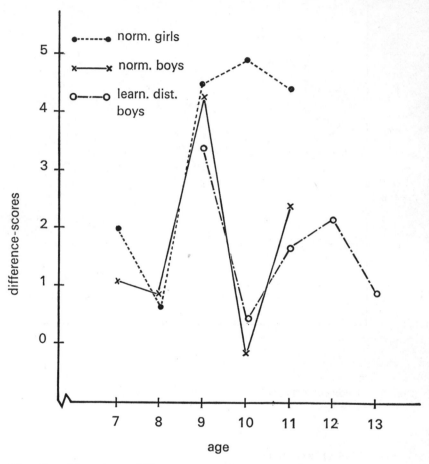

Fig. 10. Mean input difference-scores by group and age

The difference-scores of normal girls appear to become higher with increasing age ($F = 2.70$; $df = 4,45$; $p < .05$), whereas such a relation could not be shown for normal ($F = 1.58$; $df = 4,45$; $p > .10$) and learning-disturbed boys ($F = 1.30$; $df = 4,70$; $p > .25$).

5. SUMMARY AND DISCUSSION

In conformity with hypotheses I and VII temporal series of letters appear to be perceived and retained better by older than by younger children and also better by younger girls than by younger boys.

The TOP-age relation is stronger in normal than in learning-disturbed children (Hypotheses II and III). The correlation ratio of this relation appears to be $+.56$ with the normal and $+.47$ with the learning-disturbed children. The nature of the TOP-age relation in normal and reading-disturbed children is also different; in the former group the relation has besides a linear component (boys: $F = 120.20$; $df = 1,45$; p $<.001$; girls: $F = 22.38$; $df = 1,45$; $p <.001$) also a square one (boys: $F = 19.59$; $df = 1,45$; $p <.001$; girls: $F = 8.31$; $df = 1,45$; $p <.01$), whereas in the learning-disturbed children only a linear component was found ($F = 35.42$; $df = 1,70$; $p <.01$). Fig. 8 shows that the square component in the TOP-age relation in normal children must be attributed to a levelling-off of the curves after the age of 9 and with regard to the haptic curve, after the age of 8. Such a levelling off is not visible, as is shown in Fig. 9, in the group of learning-disturbed children.

One may suppose that the square component in the TOP-age relation in normal children is based on an artifact. For after the age of 9 the results reach a ceiling because no further improvement of performances could be measured. A counter-argument, however, may be put forward. the haptic curve, too, shows a strong levelling-off without anything like a ceiling occurring.

An interesting datum is that 7- and 8-year-old girls give better performances than boys at these ages. The sex difference cannot be attributed to a difference in intelligence between the two groups: the average IQs at these ages appear to be equal (108). If TOP is a conditioning factor in reading ability, then girls seem in this respect to be better equipped than boys when entering the elementary school (see also Ch. III. 4).

But more about this in the next chapter.

The prediction that the nature of the sensory input does not have any effect upon the TOP-scores has only partly come true. The performances do certainly appear to be affected by the input-channel, in the sense that both in normal and in learning-disturbed children results are considerably lower with proximal (haptic) than with telereceptive (visual and auditory) stimulation. This fact possibly reflects the proximal systems being less appropriate for temporal operations than the telereceptive systems. An alternative explanation may be that the 'supra-modal features' especially with a haptic presentation of the letters have been used less than was supposed. The experimental procedure might have occasioned this: the *S*s were not allowed to name the letters either during the stimulation phase or during the reconstruction phase. It is possible that this verbal abstraction (labelling) has hardly or not at all taken place with the processing of haptic information, but it has with the processing of visual and auditory information.

This suggests a different nature in the proximo- and telereceptive systems: the proximity-perceivers lend themselves less than the distance-perceivers to intervention of symbolic processes in the immediate stimulus-field. In the course of development behaviour becomes less dependent on the stimulus field and symbolic intervention increases in this field (Wohlwill, 1968). Parallel to and possibly also partly conditioning this development is an alteration in the hierarchical constellation of the sensory systems: the relative preference for the proximal systems at an early age makes way for a dominance of the telereceptive apparatum at a later age (Renshaw, 1930; Birch, 1962; White, 1965). Fig. 6 shows a strong levelling-off of the haptic curve of the girls after the age of 8 and – to a lesser extent – of that of the boys after the age of 10. We may see here the reflection of the decreased relative preference for the haptic-receptive system, which evidently sets in earlier with normal girls than with normal boys, whereas with learning-disturbed boys nothing of a levelling-off can be observed (Fig. 9).

A levelling-off is also present in the visual and auditory curves, but not to the same extent as in the haptic curve. Moreover, the bend in the tele-receptive curve may be interpreted as an asymptotic approximation of the maximum performance-level.

A reflection of the differences in paths of the various curves is shown in Fig. 10, from which we learn that telereceptive dominance in girls increases with age. This is not the case with normal and learning-disturbed boys, at least not within the scope of the age level dealt with. The sex difference with regard to sensory dominance is apparently due to a decline in the preference for the haptic system, which sets in at an earlier time in girls than in boys.

V. Investigations into temporal order perception: Relations to reading ability in normal and learning-disturbed children

1. INTRODUCTION

This chapter deals with the TOP-reading relation in normal and learning-disturbed children. The hypotheses IV, V and VI (Ch. II.8) will be tested. The investigations that need to be discussed have been composed in such a way that the conditions for and the nature of the TOP-reading relations can be seen more clearly.

The investigation involved the same samples as mentioned in the preceding chapter: normal boys and girls at the ages of 7 to 11 and learning-disturbed boys at the ages of 9 to 13. TOP was made operational and measured with series of letters which were presented visually, haptically and auditorily (Ch. IV. 2). Reading ability was determined by means of a test (Ch. V.2) which appeals to mechanic reading ability.

The hypotheses IV and V predict a TOP-reading relation in normal and reading-disturbed children, respectively. It remains to be seen, however, whether this relation is present to the same extent at *all ages* investigated. Groenendaal & Bakker (1971) found a significant TOP-reading relation in normal 7-year-old boys but not in boys of 10 years old. These authors, however, examined temporal perception with meaningful figures. In the present investigation this is done with letters. Meaningful figures, though verbally codifiable, are not verbal in nature; but the latter is true of letters. Reading, being a verbal process, is simulated more by the temporal perception of letters than of figures. On this basis a strong TOP-reading relation is expected at *all* ages investigated. Additional support for this prediction is provided by the results of an investigation by Senf (1969, Ch. II.3). He found a correlation between TOP and reading ability (between modality condition) in older children (15 years of age). One will remember that Senf presented temporal sequences of digits, i.e. verbal stimuli.

An interesting question with an answer that is not easy to predict, is whether TOP will correlate with reading in *girls* to the same extent as in *boys*. DeHirsch, Jansky & Langford (1966) found that the ability to re-produce tapped-out patterns predicts the reading ability of girls better than that of boys. Their investigation concerned, however, a small group of comparatively young children (1st and 2nd form primary school). Other investigations in this field are not known to us. Many studies are made with the help of boys exclusively. This is hardly surprising, when one realizes that often normal and disturbed readers are compared and that mainly boys belong to the latter category.

At first we expected a TOP-reading relation regardless of the nature of the *sensory input*. It was reasoned that letters are verbal in nature and that this verbal character is their supra-modal feature. In other words, A will be recognized as the letter A, irrespective as to whether this A is seen, felt or heard. Yet the question is whether the TOP-reading relation will be as strong under each of the sensory conditions. This doubt arises on account of the nature of the TOP-age relations such as they have been described in the preceding chapter. One will remember that the TOP-age relation with a telereceptive (visual and auditory) input rather differed from the one with a haptic input. A haptic presentation of the letters appears to cause most difficulties, especially at the older ages. The comparative difficulty of the task with a haptic input is possibly con-nected with the fact that in this case the recognition of for instance an A as the *letter* A takes longer than with a visual and auditory input. The re-ception-duration is longer which may further the process of forgetting the temporal sequence. With a haptic presentation, moreover, the concrete thing-character of the letters may be stimulated so that the verbal features of the stimuli are less called on. Also with a visual input the assumed nega-tion of the verbal character of the stimuli is possible. With an auditory input, on the contrary, such a negation is not possible.

Now reading is obviously a verbal process. Against these backgrounds it would be explicable why the TOP-reading relation is strongest with a telereceptive and especially an auditory input and less strong with a haptic input. Not contradictory to this line of thought is the fact that with 5- to 8-year-old children a test like TOAV (Ch. III) correlates with reading ability to a higher degree than TOVV. The former test implies an auditory input by which *S* cannot but perceive and retain the spoken words. With TOVV – the figures are seen and not named aloud – a verbal-ization is not strictly necessary. So verbal processes are inherent to both TOAV and reading, which is not certain in respect of TOVV. This explains the fact that more common variance with reading is shown by TOAV than by TOVV.

2. METHOD

Subjects, material and procedure. The samples have been described in Ch. IV. Therefore only a short recapitulation. Hundred children of normal primary schools participated in the investigation, 50 boys and 50 girls in age varying from 7 to 11. Also 75 learning- (reading-) disturbed boys of 9 to 13 years old.

TOP was determined by means of letters which were presented visually, haptically and auditorily, in temporal succession. After presentation of a series *S* had to indicate the serial number of two letters of this series.

Of all *S*s reading ability (Wiegersma, 1958) and IQ were determined. The IQs were computed by means of 4 WISC subtests. These subtests, viz. Similarities, Arithmetic, Picture Arrangement and Object Assembly, are recommended by Clements (1965) as acceptable substitutions for the complete battery.

Research designs. The results have been analysed by means of analyses of variance. Reading ability, age and IQ have been treated as independent variables and TOP as a dependent variable under each of the input conditions. Reading ability and not TOP was treated as an independent variable because it was easier to make the former independent of age than the latter. In order to preclude mutual dependence between reading ability and age the reading ability scores were made independent of age in the following way. On the ground of his reading score it was determined which form level (referring to Category II of Wiegersma, 1958) an *S* scored. This level was divided by the number of the form *S* actually belonged to. An example. Suppose an *S* obtains a reading score of 35. This is the level 'promotion second form' which may be rendered as 2.12, i.e. 2 years and 12 months equals 36 months. Suppose also that the *S* concerned belongs to the category of 7- to 8-year-olds. All children of this age category are supposed to be second formers. The test was carried out in the autumn, so at the time of investigation *S*s had been second formers for about 2 months. So the form of 7- to 8-year-olds was scored as 2.2, i.e. 2 years and 2 months equals 26 months. The score obtained by *S* in question consequently is 36/26 equals 1.38.

Each of the three independent variables was classified in two categories viz. above-average and below-average reading ability (AARA and BARA), IQ (AAIQ and BAIQ) and age (AAAG and BAAG). These classifications occurred irrespective of each other and in each classification the median of the scores was used as the cut-off point. As was expected reading ability and IQ did not turn out to be independent variables. This manifested itself in unequal cell frequencies. In order to obtain statistical independency of the variables mentioned, the cell frequencies were made (by omitting at random a number of data) optimally proportional to the marginal totals (Ferguson, 1966). In this way the loss of degrees of freedom is reduced to a minimum.

The analyses of variance have been applied with the normal children and the group of learning-disturbed ones, separately. That age, too, has been inserted in the factorial design was done with a view to possible interactions of this factor with the other two independent variables. As a main factor age is not interesting at this point since it has been under discussion as such in the preceding chapter.

Moreover, analyses of variance were performed in boys and girls, separately, with reading ability and IQ as independent variables and with TOP under each of the sensory conditions as a dependent variable. So sex was dealt with separately, since this factor could not very well be inserted together with reading ability, age and IQ in a $2 \times 2 \times 2 \times 2$ design since too low cell frequencies would be left in this case.

The TOP-differences have been studied *within* the group of normal and the group of reading-disturbed children as well as *between* these groups. Normal children of 9, 10 and 11 years old have been compared with reading-disturbed children of their age with respect to their TOP-scores.

3. RESULTS

TOP and reading in normal children. In this group three analyses of variance were performed; one on all children with reading ability, age and IQ as independent variables, the second and third on boys and girls respectively with reading ability and IQ as independent variables. In all three analyses TOP functioned as a dependent variable under each of the sensory conditions.

In the first analysis reading ability and IQ appeared to cause significant variance in the haptic (reading ability: $F = 4.82$; $df = 1,56$; $p < .05$; IQ: $F = 10.08$; $df = 1,56$; $p < .005$) and auditory (reading ability: $F = 7.45$; $df = 1,56$; $p < .01$; IQ: $F = 7.43$; $df = 1,56$; $p < .01$) TOP-scores, but not in the visual ones (p-values $> .10$). Age is significantly related to the visual ($F = 21.11$; $df = 1,56$; $p < .001$), the haptic ($F = 16.06$; $df = 1,56$; $p < .001$) and the auditory ($F = 35.75$; $df = 1,56$; $p < .001$) TOP-scores. But this was already known (Ch. IV). None of the interactions appeared to be significant (p-values $> .10$). Fig. 11 shows the mean TOP-scores for the two reading ability and IQ groups under each of the sensory input conditions.

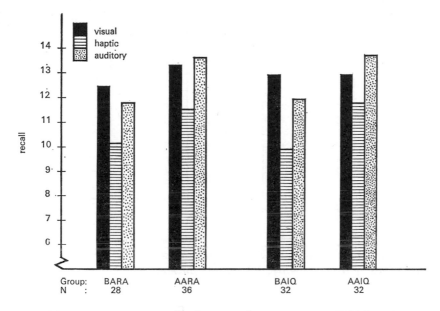

Fig. 11. Mean correct recall of temporal sequences across ages and sexes by modality, reading ability and IQ for normal children

For the *boys* the analysis of variance with reading ability and IQ as independent variables, gave the following results. Under the haptic and auditory condition the factor reading ability appeared to be significant (haptic: $F = 4.26$; $df = 1,24$; $p < .05$ and auditory: $F = 5.92$; $df = 1,24$; $p < .025$); under the visual condition the 5% level was not quite reached ($F = 3.95$; $df = 1,24$; $p < .10$). The IQ (p-values $>.10$) and the reading ability × IQ interaction (p-values $>.25$) did not appear to be significant under any of the sensory input conditions.

The same analysis gave entirely different results with *girls*. Reading ability was not related to significant variance in the TOP-scores (p-values $>.25$) under any input condition. The same holds good for the reading ability × IQ interaction (p-values $>.25$). Under the haptic condition IQ appeared to be significantly related to TOP ($F = 4.57$; $df = 1,28$; $p < .05$), but not under the visual and auditory condition (p-values $>.25$). Fig. 12 renders the results graphically viz. across modality in order to bring out the sex differences clearly.

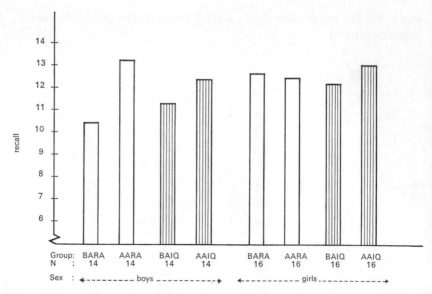

Fig. 12. Mean correct recall of temporal sequences across ages and modalities by reading ability, IQ and sex for normal children

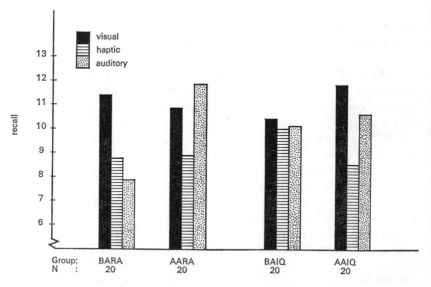

Fig. 13. Mean correct recall of temporal sequences across ages by modality, reading ability and IQ for learning-disturbed boys

54

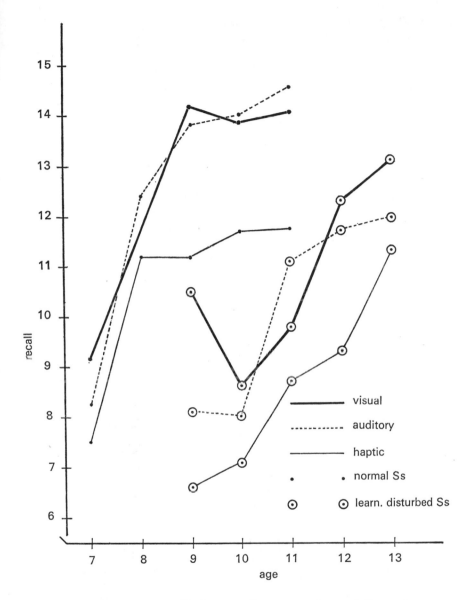

Fig. 14.   Mean correct recall of temporal sequences by modality and age for normal children (across sexes) and for learning-disturbed boys.

TOP and reading in learning-disturbed boys. Reading ability and IQ proved to be significantly related to the auditory (reading ability: $F = 34.93$; $df = 1,32$; $p < .001$; IQ: $F = 4.91$; $df = 1,32$; $p < .05$) but not to the visual and haptic TOP-scores (reading ability: p-values $> .25$; IQ: p-values $> .05$). We know already (Ch. IV) that age causes significant variance in the TOP-scores under each of the sensory conditions (visual: $F = 12.46$; $df = 1,32$; $p < .005$; haptic: $F = 10.14$; $df = 1,32$; $p < .005$ and auditory: $F = 20.90$; $df = 1,32$; $p < .001$). None of the interactions appeared to be significant (p-values $> .05$). In Fig. 13 the mean TOP-scores per reading ability and IQ group have been drawn.

TOP and reading: normal vs. learning-disturbed children. The Figures 8 and 9 have been combined in Fig. 14. This Figure makes evident that the reading-disturbed compared with the normal children are retarded in TOP-development in the course of a few years.

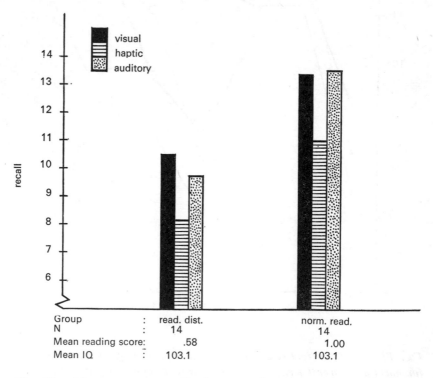

Fig. 15. *Mean correct recall of temporal sequences by modality for normal and learning-disturbed boys at ages 9-11*

At the age of 9 the reading-disturbed children present a level that normal children have reached when 7 or 8 years old; at the age of 13 retardation appears to have developed into 4 to 5 years (except for the haptic condition).

Normal children give considerably better TOP-scores at the comparative ages of 9, 10 and 11 years than the learning-disturbed boys. The z-values of the differences between the two male-groups of these ages are respectively $z = 5.03$ ($p < .001$) under the visual, $z = 5.48$ ($p < .001$) under the haptic and $z = 5.41$ ($p < .001$) under the auditory condition. But besides in reading ability these groups differ considerably in IQ as well: the mean IQ of the normal boys appears to be 112 and that of the learning-disturbed boys 95.

In order to eliminate intelligence as a possible confounding variable 14 reading-disturbed boys and the same number of normal boys were individually matched in respect of their IQ (mean IQ of the two groups 103). After this procedure the two groups appear to differ significantly as regards reading ability ($z = 3.66$; $p < .001$). Also after elimination of the IQ-differences the normal boys appear to give better (Mann Whitney Test) visual ($z = 2.41$; $p < .01$), better haptic ($z = 2.28$; $p < .025$) and better auditory ($z = 2.76$; $p < .005$) TOP-scores than the learning-(reading-) disturbed boys. In Fig. 15 the mean TOP-scores under each of the sensory conditions have been rendered per group.

4. ADDITIONAL RESULTS

Earlier (Ch. IV) mention is made of the fact that both the normal and learning-disturbed children of the ages investigated have a telereceptive dominance. This appears from the fact that the TOP-scores generally are higher with a telereceptive input (visual and auditory) than with a proximal input (haptic).

There are indications that reading ability is positively related to the degree of telereceptive dominance (Birch, 1962; Bakker, 1966 & 1967b). The visual minus haptic scores and the auditory minus haptic ones may serve as measures for visual and auditory sensory dominance, respectively. The correlations between these intra-individual differences and the reading ability-scores have been calculated for the normal and learning-disturbed children separately. The coefficients found in Table 2 are not high and insignificant except for the auditory minus haptic scores with learning-disturbed boys.

Table 2. Correlation coefficients of the relations between sensory dominance and reading ability.

	Reading ability: Normal Ss	Reading ability: Learning disturbed Ss
Visual minus haptic	—.13	+.12
Auditory minus haptic	+.15	+.44
N	100	75

5% level of significance with N = 100: r = .16, with N = 75: r = .19.
1% level of significance with N = 100: r = .23, with N = 75: r = .27.

The telereceptive dominance-scores have also been determined in the said 14 normal and 14 learning-disturbed boys (who were matched individually with the normal children as to IQ) at the age of 9 to 11. The auditory and visual dominance-scores generally appear to be *lower* in the (learning-)reading-disturbed boys than in the normal boys; the z-values (Wilcoxon Matched Pairs) of the differences, however, are not significant (visual minus haptic: $z = .62$; $p > .25$ and auditory minus haptic: $z = .81$; $p > .10$).

5. SUMMARY AND DISCUSSION

Most striking as a result is the fact that with normal girls a TOP-reading relation could not be determined under any sensory input condition or at any age. In normal boys, on the contrary, this relation obviously presents itself, especially with an auditory presentation of the temporally ordered material. Under this input the TOP-reading relation in learning-disturbed boys is even strong.

It has further appeared that TOP differentiates between normal and learning-disturbed boys under each of the three sensory conditions.

Age and IQ were not found to interact with the TOP-reading relations.

A TOP-IQ relation was found with the normal boys, but not with the learning-disturbed boys, given an auditory input. The normal girls showed this relation only with a haptic information input.

In Table 3 the results have been rendered schematically.

The fact that TOP is related to the reading ability of boys but not to that of girls asks for an explanation. If we may speak of a conditioning factor it is difficult to understand why the temporal perception with regard to the

58

Table 3. Summary of results: Levels ($< 5\%$) of significance (in %) of differences between groups.

		Normal			Learn. Dist.	Norm. vs. Dist.
		boys	girls	both	boys	boys
Conditions		(BA vs. AA)	(BA vs. AA)	(BA vs. AA)	(BA vs. AA)	boys
Reading Ability	Visual	–	–	–	–	1
	Haptic	5	–	5	–	2.5
	Auditory	2.5	–	1	.1	.5
IQ	Visual	–	–	–	–	
	Haptic	–	5	.5	–	
	Auditory	–	–	1	5	

reading ability of boys does function as such but does not with regard to the reading ability of girls.

A starting point for the explanation of the phenomenon is found in the postulate of a critical period in which the temporal perception affects the reading process. The critical character of this period, which has an upper limit only, may be determined by the capacity of temporal perception. When this capacity is below a certain level (the *threshold*) the learning-to-read process is (or: other factors conditioning this process are) affected by it.

A second assumption is that this threshold is crossed by the greater part of the girls at an earlier age than by boys: by girls mainly in the pre-school period (4 to 6 years of age) and by boys in the primary school period (6 to 8 years of age).

A direct consequence of this line of thought is that girls in their post-critical period (6 to 8) have a better temporal perception than boys. This is precisely what the results (Ch. IV) indicate (Fig. 7).

So with boys the critical period seems in part to coincide with the elementary learning-to-read process (age 6 to 8), whereas this phase with girls is present before the beginning of this learning process (until 6 years of age). The fact that the *actual* TOP-scores of boys of the primary school are connected with their reading ability but not those of girls, is then intelligible.

This does not imply, however, that the reading ability of primary-school-girls has not been affected by their temporal order capacity. Only, with girls one should not think of an actual effect but of a post-effect. Or putting it differently: some boys of the elementary school read badly because among other things their temporal ordering *is* bad, but some girls read badly because their temporal ordering *has been* bad.

It is conceivable that the coinciding of the critical period with the elementary learning-to-read process may have more dramatic consequences than when this period, as is the case with girls, precedes the actual learning-to-read process. In the first case there is a direct interaction between (poor) temporal perception and reading, in the second case TOP probably interacts with factors conditioning the actual reading process.

It may also be imagined that the TOP-reading interaction with boys is dramatic to such an extent that owing to this some of them become reading-disturbed. One consequence of this line of thought is that more boys than girls are liable to become reading-disturbed and another that reading-disturbed boys are comparatively very bad temporal-orderers. The first fact is wellknown (a.o. Eisenberg, 1966) and the second becomes evident from the present study, both in quantitative and qualitative respect. Quantitative: learning-disturbed boys differ more from normal boys than below-average readers from above-average readers within the group of normal boys. Qualitative: learning-disturbed boys and normal ones do not only differ in TOP-scores with an auditory and haptic input, such as the below-average and above-average reading normal boys, but also with a visual input.

The 'threshold model' that has been discussed, leads to a number of predictions. One of these is that a TOP-reading relation is really present with comparatively young girls. Generally, girls from the first form of the elementary school are not far beyond the critical period. A certain influence of that period upon their reading ability may therefore be expected. With regard to this prediction the data mentioned by De-Hirsch, Jansky & Langford (1966) are relevant. The ability of nursery-school children to imitate rhythmic patterns appeared to predict the reading ability of girls in the first two grades of the primary school but not that of boys, or at least so to a much lesser extent.

The investigation mentioned in Ch. III is also relevant. Nursery-school children, about 200 girls and 200 boys, 5 to 6 years of age, were tested in TOVV and TOAV. In the first and second form of the primary school the reading ability of these children was determined. Of the two tests TOVV is best comparable to the method of TOP-investigation described in this chapter.

Twenty boys and 20 girls, being a random sample out of the total random sample of about 400 children, were involved in order to examine the prediction that TOP and reading are related in girls at comparatively young ages. On the ground of the median of the TOVV-scores girls and

60

boys were divided in above-average and below-average temporal order perceivers. The reading ability-scores belonging to each group were compared and statistically analysed (Mann-Whitney Test). The results have been rendered in Table 4.

In conformity with the prediction the reading ability of girls belonging to the first form appears to be related to TOVV of a year earlier. The reading ability of the same girls when in the second form is not significantly related to TOVV. The reading ability of boys, on the other hand, does not at all correlate with their pre-school TOVV-scores. The latter result may in part be attributed to a smaller variability of these scores in boys than in girls (boys: mean TOVV-score of the below-average group 2.3, and of the above-average group 4.7; girls: mean TOVV-score of the below-average group 2.0 and of the above-average group 5.7).

With regard to the boys a different result would indeed be expected on the ground of the postulated threshold model. For their reading ability, too, ought to correlate with pre-school TOP-scores. The critical period is considered, surely, to be determined by the TOP-capacity. If this is small, as is the case with many boys below the age of 6 to 8 and with many girls below the age of 4 to 6, a TOP-effect upon reading may be expected according to the model. Now in the investigation under discussion the TOVV-scores of boys certainly are not any higher than those of girls. The TOVV-scores of the girls are evidently below the threshold value in view of their relation with reading ability. But then this also will hold good for the TOVV-scores of the boys, and therefore in them, too, a TOVV-reading relation is expected. This prediction has not become evident.

This result of the boys may be explained, however, by the following alternative model of the one just described. The essential point of the alternative model is a disconnection of the critical period and the critical TOP-capacity. The postulate of a critical period in which temporal order perception affects the learning-to-read process remains, but this phase is not determined by a TOP-threshold. This alternative model simply postulates a critical period of age, within which TOP does but outside which TOP does not interact with the learning-to-read process, regardless of the TOP capacity level. With girls this phase is thought to occur between the 4th and 6th and with boys between the 6th and 8th year. Within this model pre-school temporal order perception does not have any effect upon the learning-to-read process with boys, but with girls it does. On the reverse, temporal order perception of primary school girls does not have any effect upon their reading ability, but it does in primary school boys.

In Fig. 16 the 'connected' (critical period *with* TOP-threshold restriction)

61

Table 4. *Effects of pre-school TOP on reading ability of boys and girls in the 1st and 2nd form of the primary school*

| | Reading ability: Form 1 | | | | Reading ability: Form 2 | | | |
| | Boys | | Girls | | Boys | | Girls | |
	Test I[1]	Test II[2]	Test I	Test II	Test I	Test II	Test I	Test II
a) Below-average TOVV	19.1	28.4	11.6	17.3	30.1	50.4	26.6	46.2
a) Above-average TOVV	15.1	28.4	22.4	33.8	27.8	45.8	34.3	56.8
z	.80	.15	2.28	2.62	.20	.49	1.18	1.25
p	> .10	> .25	< .025	< .005	> .25	> .25	< .25	< .25
N	20	20	20	20	19	19	20	20

1. Wiegersma, 1958.
2. Brus, B. *Een-minuut-test*. Nijmegen: Berkhout, 1963.

a) Mean IQ of the Below-Average boys: 97; girls: 100.
   Mean IQ of the Above-Average boys: 101; girls: 98.

and 'disconnected' (critical period *without* TOP-threshold restriction) models have been rendered schematically.

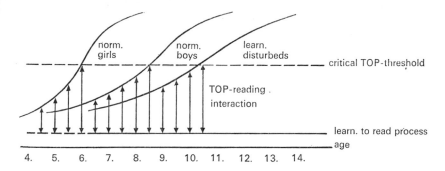

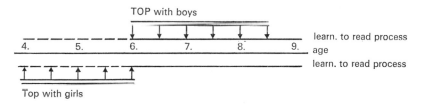

Fig. 16. Critical-phase models. Above coupled (threshold) model; below uncoupled model

Both models postulate a life period during which temporal order perception and reading *functionally interact*. This postulation is based on the presence of TOP-reading relations during the critical periods.

In view of yet another explanation of the facts two things should be remembered. First, the failure to show a correlation does not mean that a correlation does not exist. Secondly, the degree of correlation is among other things dependent on the variability of the scores obtained. A large variability generally heightens the degree of correlation. With this in mind one may argue that during a critical or sensitive period the variability of scores should be relatively large. For in such a period not all Ss perform at the same level: the period will be reached by some Ss but not quite by others. Thus there will be individual differences in maturation that will provide for a wide range of scores (Pelle, 1967). On account of increased variability of scores during a critical period the degree of correlation will

63

be heightened. Outside of such periods, however, variability will be relatively low so that correlations between variables are low too.

What are the facts? Above (Ch. V.5) a study on the relation of TOVV and reading was mentioned. With girls of 5 to 6 years old TOVV appeared to correlate with reading ability, while with boys such a relation could not be established. The 'variability model' described just now would predict a larger variability in the TOVV-scores of girls than in those of boys given that TOVV-development is in a critical period with girls but not (yet) with boys of these ages. The TOVV-scores of girls really appeared to vary more than those of boys.

At later ages (7 to 8) it was found that TOP of boys and not of girls is related to reading ability (Ch. V.3; Table 3). If this finding is due to the fact that the boys but not the girls are in a critical period of TOP-development the variability model predicts larger variability in the TOP-scores of boys than of girls. Again this appears to be the case: the means of the below-average and the above-average TOP-scores (auditory input) differ more with boys (BA: 8.0; AA: 15.4) than with girls (BA: 10.5; AA: 15.2).

The differences in variability that were found are not sufficient to explain the phenomena, however. These differences can explain *differences* in degree of correlation but not *absence* of correlation. The latter was found in some samples mentioned above in spite of variability of messurings being present.

The three models discussed have the postulation of a critical period in common. The 'connected' and 'disconnected' models assume a functional TOP-reading interaction during a particular life-period but not outside it. The 'variability' model unconditionally predicts a TOP-reading relation but adds that the relation is most evident when the development of either TOP or reading is in a critical period. None of the models can account for all the facts. Therefore, it is difficult to determine which of them should be preferred. For the time being, however, it is important to know that a number of data suggests the correctness of some critical period model.

The terms critical and sensitive periods are merely terms to indicate that a phenomenon occurs in a certain phase of development and not or less so in another one. Sluckin (1970) states that sensitive periods are 'those stages in development when the organism is especially susceptible to environmental influences' (p. 66). It is assumed that during these periods patterns of neurophysiological changes facilitate certain forms of behaviour (Scott, 1958; Caldwell, 1962). In the present study the TOP-reading interaction is assumed to be facilitated by such organic changes. Nowadays one can only speculate as to the causes and nature of these changes, however.

Another outcome of the present investigation is that the TOP-reading relation appears to be strongest with an auditory input especially in reading-disturbed children. This result may be connected with the fact that with this modal presentation the label is offered at the same time. In other words, with an auditory input one *cannot but* assimilate the phonemes. It has been noticed earlier that with a visual and a haptic presentation labelling of the stimuli is not strictly necessary. Partly owing to application of the reconstruction method the temporal ordering task may under these conditions also be performed purely perceptually, i.e. without verbal participation.

Especially learning-disturbed boys may have proceeded in this way. For particularly in them any connection between TOP and reading is absent with a visual and haptic input whereas the relation is very strongly present with an auditory input; and the verbal label is certainly not to be neglected in this.

If this supposition of the verbal and perceptual conception of the task is sound this probably has consequences for the validity of the sensory dominance concept. Especially in the learning-disturbed boys the auditory minus haptic TOP scores appeared to correlate with reading ability to a substantial degree (Table 2). These intra-individual difference-scores are a measure indeed for sensory dominance, in the present case auditory dominance. However, one may ask the question what matters here most, an auditory or a verbal dominance. If the conception of the task is verbal in nature with an auditory input and perceptual with a haptic input, the auditory minus haptic scores probably do not so much imply a sensory as a verbal (versus perceptual) dominance.

The validity of the concept sensory dominance therefore requires careful examination whenever made operational.

VI. Temporal order perception: Summary and discussion of major findings

A great number of investigations concerning the perception and retention of temporal order have now been reviewed. Consequently a provisional assessment of the results can be made.

Apparently the temporal order concept may be operationally defined in various ways. In some investigations S has to explicate the temporal order (Hirsh & Sherrick, 1961; Efron, 1963; Lowe & Campbell, 1965; Bakker, 1967a & 1969; and others). In explication the serial location of an item within series of items is asked. With other investigators explication is not required but the perception of temporal order is implied in the task, as is the case with the perception and reproduction of rhythmic patterns (Stamback, 1951; Blank, Weider & Bridger, 1968) and of series of digits (Belmont & Birch, 1966).

In the reading process *as such* temporal order is found to be produced without explication of the serial location of each letter within a word or of each word within a sentence. When the word 'kind' is read and pronounced the [i] will follow the [k], but the reader is not required to indicate that e.g. the [i] comes second in the temporal series of phonemes. In this respect a TOP-test without explication seems to simulate the learning-process better than a test with explication.

The results of investigations suggest, however, that in respect of the TOP-reading relation it is not of vital importance whether a TOP-test is operated either with or without explication.

More essential for the TOP-reading relation seem to be the concepts verbal-nonverbal. When with the perception and retention of temporal series, a verbal medium is operant as is the case with series of letters, digits and meaningful figures, the TOP-reading relation will come into play.

One might suppose that the relation exists on account of the verbal common variance of the reading- and TOP-material and that therefore the crucial point is not temporal but verbal in nature with reading-disturbed children. This hypothesis, however, seems incorrect.

An example may clarify this. Suppose a child receives in visual-temporal succession the letters O, A, I, E, U for reproduction. Two remarks in respect of this series may be made, viz. that one is here dealing with a temporal series and also that the stimuli are vowels, so verbal items. When at one time it appears that the child is not equal to the task, will this fact be inductive to the conclusion that one is dealing with a labelling problem? We may advance counterarguments. When S is asked to name the individual letters most probably this will be carried out correctly: for many reading-disturbed children this instruction is no problem at all. A second argument against the labelling hypothesis is the fact that reading-disturbed children meet with difficulties especially with an auditory presentation of series of digits. With an auditory input phonemes, so the labels themselves, are presented; S is no longer required to label. On the ground of investigations that were made we may not simply say that bad readers present verbal labelling problems.

Neither can we simply state, that their temporal perception and/or temporal retention is disturbed. If that were true a TOP-reading relation might be expected whenever series of nonverbal stimuli such as meaningless figures were presented. And this proves not to be the case (Bakker, 1967a; Groenendaal & Bakker, 1971; and others). So reading-disturbed children do not seem to present any verbal labelling problem nor any temporal ordering problem *as such* but difficulties which occur 'when verbal items are presented in a time scheme' (Bakker, 1970b, p. 96). In other words, the interaction between time and verbal code is disturbed and not so much the main factors. Senf (1969, pp. 26, 27) says practically the same when writing '...failures were generally specific to the ordering of stimuli not to their accuracy of recall'. Senf used series of digits and probably something may be said for substituting the word 'stimuli' by 'verbal stimuli' in the above quotation.

Disturbances in the temporal perception of verbal or verbally codifiable stimuli appear to occur not only in dyslexics but also in aphasics (Efron, 1963a; Lowe & Campbell, 1965). The two groups seem to have disturbances in the ordering-labelling interaction in common. Meanwhile also something else happens in aphasics: the labelling itself, too, may cause difficulties for them. So, besides the interaction of ordering and labelling also one of the main factors, viz. the labelling, may be disturbed in aphasics.

And what in case of disturbance of the other main factor, i.e. the perception or experience of the temporal order? In this case one is dealing with an anomaly which may have extreme consequences for behaviour in its totality. This prediction is connected with the fundamental character of time which plays a part not only in language but in any behaviour. A disturbance in temporal perception and/or experience would therefore mean that one had difficulty not only with the succession of phonemes but for instance also with the motorial sequence of walking. When considered in this way aphasia and dyslexia are partial disturbances whereas primary deviations in the perception and experience of temporal order have repercussions on all behaviour.

Van Meel and associates (Van Meel, 1968; Van Meel, Vlek & Bruijel, 1970) are of the opinion that learning-disturbed children show deviations in what is called the temporal integration in perception and cognition processes. According to them this disturbance has its roots in the affective-dynamic conditions of cognitive functioning. Said cognitive style is described as 'foreshortening of temporal perspective' (Van Meel *et al.*, 1970, p. 97). The contraction of the temporal perspective results into an inclination to carry out instructions in the shortest time possible.

They literally do not allow themselves any time. Therefore they are far from accurate, overlook relevant information and produce poor results. Van Meel and associates could actually demonstrate that learning-disturbed children assimilate information more and more inedequately as it becomes more complex. The point here is that Van Meel postulates a disturbance in the time-experience of learning-disturbed children. Time plays a fundamental part in any behaviour. Perception, motion, thinking, volition, feeling, all these processes are not well possible without temporal participation. With a disturbance in the temporal functioning consequences for the behaviour in its totality are expected and not only consequences for the perception and processing of information. Time conditions all functions of an organism. If this is correct learning-disturbed children are threatened by a disturbance in the experience of time not only as to thinking (Van Meel's publication of 1968 is entitled 'threatened thinking' – transl. –), but as to their entire behaviour. Further investigation will have to decide if this is really the case.

We shall further enter into the problem of time and temporal order in the following chapter.

The TOP-reading relation does not appear to be the same under every input-condition. It is true, TOP differentiates *between* normal and reading-disturbed children under all input-conditions, but this does not hold good in respect of below-average and above-average readers *within* the group of normal and learning-disturbed boys.

In general auditory-temporal series are strongest related with reading ability. As was noted earlier (Ch. V.5) an explanation is the fact that with an auditory presentation the verbal label is offered so that *S cannot but* work with this label. With a haptic but also with a visual presentation of the stimulus-material and the subsequent response by means of a re-construction-method, this is not necessarily the case. Investigations in which response is required either with or without application of a re-construction-method might shed some light on this problem.

If the perception, retention and reproduction of auditory-temporal patterns is difficult for dyslexics, even more difficult for them is the repro-duction of verbal stimuli presented two by two (of each pair one digit visually and at the same time one digit auditorily – Senf, 1969). What matters besides the perception and retention of temporal order in such a bisensory process is the integration of simultaneoulsy presented visual and auditory information. As Senf's results proved, the integration-aspect makes TOP a strong variable, differentiating between good and bad readers.

Intersensory integration is also an important moment in the BB-test by Birch & Belmont (1964, 1965). In this test auditory dot patterns are to be matched with visual ones. But the visual information in the BB-test is unlike in Senf's not presented simultaneously but subsequently to the auditory information. In spite of this difference the BB-test, too, appears to discriminate strongly between good and bad readers.

Remarkable in Senf's results was that it was harder to retain the se-quences with comparatively long inter-pair intervals. The differences be-tween the reading-groups were greater with intervals of 2 sec. than with intervals of 0.5 sec. Muller & Bakker (1968) used comparatively short inter-vals (.75 Msec.) in their investigation, whereas in other experiments (Bakker, 1967a; Groenendaal & Bakker, 1971) long intervals (2 to 4 sec.) were used. In all cases TOP appeared to differentiate between the reading groups. It could not be decided whether long interstimulus-intervals (ISI) produced any more effect than short ones because different samples were involved.

The problem, however, is important enough. By varying the ISI's conclusions can be drawn concerning the nature of the temporal memory of disturbed and normal readers. Senf's results make us suppose that the memory of reading-disturbed boys can bridge only a comparatively brief space of time. This hypothesis is among other things inductive to the prediction that there is a relation between reading ability and the ability to synthesize words which are presented temporally fractionized. In a number of investigations this relation was actually demonstrated (Monsees, 1968; Conners, Kramer & Guerra, 1969).

Probably the most conspicuous result of the investigations that have been described is the effect of sex upon TOP and the TOP-reading relation.

At younger ages (5 to 8) girls appear to give better TOP-scores than boys. This has become evident by investigations with both nursery-school children (Ch. III) and primary school children (Ch. IV).

Moreover, temporal order perception appears to condition reading ability, but with girls at a different point of time than with boys. With girls a relation was discovered between TOP, defined at nursery-school, and reading ability in the primary forms of the elementary school (Ch. V; DeHirsch, Jansky & Langford, 1966), but not so with boys. At a later age, however, TOP correlates with the reading ability of boys and not with that of girls. These findings have led to the construction of a model in which a critical TOP-reading interaction period, either connected or not connected to a critical TOP-capacity, is present in girls at an earlier age (pre-school period mainly) than in boys (primary school period mainly).

In the preceding chapter it was suggested that critical periods originate from neurophysiological changes in the organism. As to the critical period for TOP-reading interaction these changes apparently set in with girls earlier than with boys. One can only speculate about the nature of the changes.

With regard to the TOP-reading interaction period they are possibly connected with lateral differentiations of brain functions. That in the vast majority of cases reading is primarily dependent on the functioning of the left hemisphere is an established fact. This dependency increases with age. Possibly TOP goes through a similar neuropsychological development.

The following chapter deals with this problem. Then in the last chapter an attempt will be made to integrate the findings of cerebral TOP lateralization and neuropsychological conceptions of reading.

VII. Hemispheric specializations in temporal order perception

1. INTRODUCTION

'I am very much interested in this question raised by Dr. Hirsh as to whether the temporal lobe is the temporal lobe or the verbal lobe. Dr. Milner's data appear to suggest that the left temporal lobe is the verbal lobe and the right temporal lobe is the temporal lobe. There is, however, an apparent conflict between her data and those of Dr. Efron'. Thus wrote Masland when discussing a paper by Milner on 'Brain mechanisms suggested by studies of temporal lobes' (Milner, 1967, p. 141).

Milner gave an account of the effects occurring in lesions of the left and right temporal lobes. From her investigation it became evident that patients with a right temporal lobectomy score post-operatively lower than pre-operatively on the Seashore Tonal Memory Test. On the other hand no post- and pre-operative differences were found in patients who had undergone left temporal lobectomy. With the Tonal Memory Test a short sequence of tones is played twice and S has to indicate of which tone the pitch is altered in the second presentation.

It had been determined beforehand that simple pitch discrimination is not affected by the lesions. It is therefore evident that the perception of auditory-*temporal* patterns is disturbed by lesions of the right temporal lobe. From other investigations it appeared that the visual- and proprioceptive-temporal perception in these patients is also disturbed.

On the ground of Milner's results it is natural to conclude that temporal order perception is mediated by the right temporal lobe and apparently not by the corresponding area of the left hemisphere.

But is this conclusion really true? Efron (1963 a, b, c and 1967) arrived at different results and conclusions than Milner. He presented to his Ss series of two stimuli. S had to indicate each time which of the stimuli was presented first. By this set-up Efron demonstrated that temporal order perception is controlled by the dominant, i.e. the language hemisphere. In nearly all cases this is the left-hemisphere. Efron could further make it plausible that especially the temporal lobe of this hemisphere mediates the perception of temporal order.

Efron's results seem to be in contradiction with Milner's. The question raised by Masland which opened this chapter is therefore to the point. It will, however, appear that the apparent contradiction is not a real one.

2. NEUROPSYCHOLOGICAL EXPERIMENTS IN THE LINE OF EFRON

The experiments by Efron show much similarity with those by Hirsh (1959) and Hirsh & Sherrick (1961). The latter authors make a distinction between the perception of temporal order and the perception of succession. With succession it is a matter of discriminating between simultaneous and dissimultaneous appearance of two or more stimuli. Temporal order concerns the sequence in which two or more dissimultaneous stimuli appear.

Suppose that S1 appears at moment t1 and S2 at moment t2. When the interval t2–t1 becomes shorter there will be an instant at which S1 and S2 are thought to be presented simultaneously. When subsequently the interval becomes longer one will perceive succession, so dissimultaneity of S1 and S2. Determination of succession does not imply, however, that the sequence has been determined. With sequence the question is which stimulus, S1 or S2, appeared first and which last in succession.

Hirsh & Sherrick point out that S1 and S2 have to be different in order to make perception of sequential order possible. If S1 and S2 are, for instance, both flashes of light and S1 is red then S2 should have a different colour. Only in that case can the question which stimulus appeared first be answered. Identical stimuli can be used when the discrimination to be made is one between simultaneity and succession, unidentical stimuli are necessary for the investigation of temporal order.

Hirsh & Sherrick found that an interstimulus interval (ISI) of 20 Msec. is sufficient for the determination of *sequential order*. This applies to stimuli that are auditory, visual, tactile as well as bimodal. Untrained Ss require longer ISI's, however, as appeared from later research (Hirsh & Fraisse, 1964; Gengel & Hirsh, 1970). *Succession* of auditory stimuli is perceived with ISI's as short as 2 Msec. For visual and tactile stimuli these ISI's are higher, but they are generally lower than the ISI's necessary for the perception of temporal order.

The perception of succession and of temporal order are apparently different phenomena. A number of differences have already emerged. Temporal order perception for instance presumes that the stimuli are different so that each of them can be identified, a condition which is not

72

required for the perception of succession. Possibly as a result of this, longer ISI's are required for temporal order perception than for the perception of succession. A remarkable difference is also that the ISI's required with succession are dependent on the modal input, which is not the case with the perception of temporal order.

Also from another fact it appears that succession and temporal order are phenomena with different roots. For Efron (1963a), Lowe & Campbell (1965) but others, too, have shown that temporal order perception does but the perception of succession does not discriminate between normal and aphasic patients. This difference may perhaps be attributed to the fact that sequence perception presumes the individual identification of the stimuli whereas succession does not.

In the investigations mentioned so far identification was possible because a separate *verbal label* could be attached to each stimulus. The response, too, was given by means of the label. Suppose that S1 is a high-pitched and S2 is a low-pitched tone. During presentation of S1 and S2 the labels 'high' and 'low' are given along with their physical qualities. The labels are produced as a vocal response: to the question which of the stimuli was presented first the answer 'high' or 'low' is given.

In said studies concerning the perception of temporal order the verbal medium plays a part and, as will become evident from subsequent arguments, probably a crucial part at that.

In one of his investigations Efron (1963b) tested the hypothesis that 'the "point in the central nervous system" where temporal discrimination is made is in the hemisphere dominant for speech' (p. 265). Efron wanted to verify this hypothesis by making it plausible that information arriving in the non-speech hemisphere (mostly the right one) is transferred to the speech hemisphere. This transfer takes time. In order to effect simultaneous arrival in the speech hemisphere of information transferred from the right hemisphere and of information already present in the left hemisphere it will be necessary to present the information that is to be transferred a little earlier. Fig. 17 renders Efron's hypothesis (1963b, p. 266) schematically. The figure shows that information originating from the left sensory surface will, according to the hypothesis, have to cover a larger distance than the information originating from the right side. On the left side the information will therefore have to be presented a little earlier if one is to affect simultaneous arrival in the speech hemisphere (left) from the two information sources. In Efron's experiment the stimuli were shocks to the right and left index finger as well as flashes of light by which the right and left nasal retina were stimulated. Since the sensible

73

paths cross, the information from the left is conducted to the right hemisphere and vice versa.

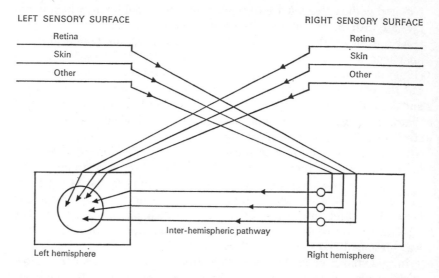

Fig. 17. 'This diagram schematically illustrates the crossed sensory pathways from the sensory receptors to the cortex. The hypothesis states that the stimuli from opposite sides of the body are compared in some region of the left hemisphere (large circle). It is considered likely that a synapse would be interposed in the pathway from right to left hemisphere (small circle).' (Efron, 1963).

As a result the fact emerged that *S*s perceive simultaneity of stimulation when stimulation on the left precedes the one on the right by about 3.5 Msec. By continued investigation this result was confirmed.

Further location of the place where temporal perception is mediated in the left hemisphere was desirable. In another investigation (Efron,1963a) visual and auditory stimuli were presented in temporal succession to both normal persons and patients with receptive and expressive aphasia. Aphasic patients appear to require longer ISI's than normal persons on the understanding that with expressive aphasia especially the temporal perception of auditory stimuli and with receptive aphasia that of visual stimuli is disturbed. A brain-damaged patient without aphasia did not show any disturbance in temporal perception. The locus where the perception of temporal order is mediated is therefore exactly the place where passive and active language are controlled: '... indeed, the defect in sequence discrimination was found only when there was some degree of aphasia present' (Efron, 1963a, p. 418).

Efron (1963, 1967) refers to a number of other studies (Hirsh & Sherrick, 1961; Halliday & Mingay, 1962; Edwards & Auger, 1965; Holmes, 1965; Lowe & Campbell, 1965) from which it appears directly or indirectly that perception of temporal order is mediated left-cerebrally. In the meantime his results have also been confirmed by Van Allen, Benton & Gordon (1966).

It should, however, be noted that all the investigators mentioned used the method of Hirsh & Sherrick. As was observed earlier this method has certain characteristics. We shall try to make it plausible that Efron and other investigators in his line obtained these results because of the characteristics referred to.

3. NEUROPSYCHOLOGICAL EXPERIMENTS IN THE LINE OF MILNER

A study by Milner was mentioned earlier in connection with the fact that she arrived at results different from Efron's. This induced Masland to ask the question which opened this chapter.

What was the case?

Milner (1962, 1967) applied the Seashore battery to patients who had undergone unilateral temporal lobectomy. In some the left, in others the right temporal lobe had been removed. The battery consists of six subtests of which Rhythm and Tonal Memory clearly appeal to the perception and retention of temporal order. With Rhythm rhythmic patterns are tapped out in quick succession and S has to indicate whether they were identical or not. With Tonal Memory a series of tones is presented twice, but in such a way that the second time one tone has been altered. S has to indicate which one.

The patients were examined pre- and post-operatively. The right temporal lobectomy cases appeared on the whole to make more errors postoperatively than pre-operatively. Patients with left lesions, on the other hand, scored pre- and post-operatively at about the same level. The largest post-operative relapse was measured with the Tonal Memory test.

Another test applied was the Stylus-Maze Learning Test. On this test, too, patients with a right lesion showed pre- vs. post-operative differences whereas those with a left lesion did not. These results occurred with visual as well as purely proprioceptive exploration of the mazes. According to

Milner the difficulties in both cases were not spatial but temporal in nature: the retention of the sequence of the turning-points in the maze.

Milner's findings were confirmed in similar patients by Chase (1967), especially with regard to the Tonal Memory Test.

Milner (1967) refers to an investigation by Shankweiler (1966a) in which temporal lobectomy cases were asked to hum traditional tunes. Patients with a right lesion scored particularly low, but patients with a left lesion did not. The production of nonverbal musical patterns, too, evidently depends on the integrity of the right hemisphere.

An investigation by Fedio & Mirsky (1969) is interesting within the scope of this discussion since children participated in it. *S*s were patients with unilateral epileptiform discharges localized to the left or right temporal lobe. The battery was composed of auditory- and visual-verbal as well as auditory- and visual-nonverbal tests. All items had to be reproduced in the same order in which they were presented. From the results it appears that left temporal cases have more difficulties with verbal-temporal tasks than right temporal cases, whereas the opposite applies with regard to nonverbal-temporal tasks.

The studies in the line of Milner that have been discussed so far were investigations in which auditory stimulation was binaural. With binaural stimulation both ears receive the same information simultaneously, a situation that is comparable with normal verbal communication. It has become evident that the processing of this information embodied in temporal patterns depends more on the right than on the left hemisphere.

Another method frequently applied is the dichotic stimulation technique. In this case different auditory-temporal patterns are presented to both ears simultaneously.

These investigations have led to the same conclusions as those in which stimulation was binaural. For in general the left ear appears to give better performances than the right, which indicates a dependency of nonverbal-temporal perception on right hemisphere functioning.

Kimura for instance showed (1964, 1967) that normal adults perceive and retain music better through the left ear than through the right ear. Spellacy (1970) and Spreen, Spellacy & Reid (1970) arrived at a similar conclusion. These authors also proved a left-ear preference for tonal patterns.

Shankweiler (1966b) and Schulhoff & Goodglass (1969) applied the dichotic technique to patients who had undergone left or right temporal lobectomy. In both studies the assimilation of tonal patterns appeared to depend more on the integrity of the right than of the left cerebral cortex.

4. LEFT *vs*. RIGHT: TEMPORAL *vs*. NONTEMPORAL OR VERBAL *vs*. NONVERBAL?

The investigations in Milner's line were in fact not set up with a view to left-right differences in temporal perception. They primarily deal with lateral differences on the line verbal-nonverbal. But tonal patterns are also temporal in nature besides being nonverbal-auditory.

The problem verbal *vs*. temporal became interesting with Efron's finding that the perception of temporal order is mediated left-cerebrally. Masland (1967) noticed a contradiction with the results obtained by Milner, since the stimulus-patterns examined, though classifiable as non-verbal-auditory, often show an inherent temporal moment as well.

On the ground of Milner's investigations the conclusion should be drawn that nonverbal processes are mediated right-cerebrally and that it is of little importance whether temporal moments are or are not inherent in these processes, just as it is of little importance whether these processes are auditory, visual or proprioceptive in nature.

Verbal processes, on the other hand, are controlled by the left hemi-sphere. That temporal moments, inherent in the verbal processes, do not alter this fact is proved not so much by Milner and her Montreal-group. This is probably due to the fact that for verbal stimulation mostly the dichotic listening-technique is used. In this case different verbal stimuli (letters, digits) are presented simultaneously to both ears and *S* then has to indicate which stimuli he has heard. In nearly all experiments *S* is free to choose the sequential order in which he reproduces the stimuli *(free recall)*. The perception of temporal order is not at all called upon. To our knowledge Clark, Knowles & Macclean (1970) have so far been the only ones who demanded ordered recall in a dichotic listening-experiment. After presentation of for instance the pairs 3/7, 8/2, and 4/9 (3, 8 and 4 to the left ear and 7, 2 and 9 to the right ear) *S* had to give 3, 8, 4 and 7, 2, 9 in response.

The investigation by Fedio & Mirsky (1969) has already been mentioned. In their experiment *ordered recall* was demanded. However, it was not so much the demand for ordered recall as the either verbal or nonverbal character of the stimulus material that appeared to decide which hemi-sphere is involved most in the processing of information.

An investigation in which stimulation was visual was carried out by Dimond (1969). The test was set up in such a way that series of digits could be projected on the left and right cortex. *Ordered recall* was de-manded. In processing the information the right cortex appeared to make more errors than the left one. This result was expected because the test was concerned with the temporal perception of verbal material.

In our laboratory a series of experiments have been performed in the last few years (Bakker, 1967c, 1968, 1969, 1970a; Bakker & Boeijenga, 1970) in which verbal (digits, letters) and nonverbal (rhythmic patterns) material was presented monaurally to normal and reading-disturbed children between the ages of 6 and 13. 'Monaurally' means separately to each ear and not simultaneously. In practically all cases *ordered recall* was demanded.

On the whole the results showed the same thing as obtained by dichotic stimulation: the left hemisphere is dominant for the processing of temporally-ordered verbal information and the right hemisphere is more appropriate for the processing of temporally-ordered nonverbal information.

Recapitulating, it may be stated that the perception of temporal order is mediated neither exclusively left- nor exclusively right-cerebrally and that it depends on the verbal or nonverbal character of the temporally ordered material which hemisphere is primarily involved in the processing of the information (Bakker, 1970b).

If this is correct the tasks set by Efron (1963 a, b, c) must have been *verbal-temporal* in nature. On the face of it this does not seem probable, for the stimuli presented by Efron were figures, flashes of light and the like.

Earlier it was noted that Efron adopted the procedures of Hirsh & Sherrick. These authors had stated that temporal perception is possible only if the stimuli can be identified separately. By means of a label the identity is fixed: 'the two events in question must be distinctive so that *O* has some way of labelling them differently and then using these labels to identify which occurred first or second' (pp. 423–424). The *S*s in Efron's investigation were in fact asked to name the stimuli. Consequently a distinct verbal moment is present in his tasks. It is therefore possible that the speech hemisphere mediates the perception of temporal order on account of this verbal aspect.

Efron himself (1963b) has also recognized this possibility. He gives an account of a delay circuit which *S* can operate himself in order to make the two stimuli (flashes of light in this case) appear simultaneously. So in this procedure *S* was not required to give a vocal response. The importance of this set-up lies, according to Efron, 'in the fact that the shift to the left was observed even when no verbal response was required' (p. 274). But, he adds '...it may still be argued that the subject must use "internal" language in his performance...' (p. 274). The risk that really internal language was used seems even greater when the *S*s who participated in this 'no-verbal response' experiment had earlier participated in investigations where a verbal response was required. Possibly the 'overt' speech in the earlier experiment has passed into 'internal' speech in the next one. Efron does not mention, however, what experiences the participants in the 'no-verbal response' experiment had already had. Mention is made of the fact that only few Ss participated in this experiment and that the investigation was stopped because of the large variability of results by which no statistical reliability could be achieved. The 'no-verbal response' procedure appeared, moreover, to be extremely fatiguing for the Ss.

If it would really appear that speech (overt or internal) mediates the perception of temporal order in Efron's experiments, this would explain much. It would explain the fact that aphasics (Efron, 1963a; Lowe & Campbell, 1965) and dyslexics (Efron, 1963a) have so much difficulty with these exercises.

It would possibly also give an explanation of the fact that aphasic children have no difficulty with a task in which time does play a part, but in which the verbal medium does not. One may think of the perception of succession. This perception does not differentiate between normal and aphasic persons (Lowe & Campbell, 1965).

But that precisely the speech hemisphere mediates the perception of temporal order would be the most important thing that would be explained by the verbal moment in Efron's tasks.

The problem is to find a set-up by means of which more certainty can be obtained as to the question whether language does or does not play an essential part as a medium in some temporal order perception tasks.

Such a procedure might be the following (Bakker, 1970b). Instead of two nameable stimuli (such as red and green light) two unnameable but yet different stimuli are presented. For instance two different meaningless figures. By means of a reconstruction-method one may have S indicate which figure was presented first and which last.

Any evidence that in such a case it is not the left hemisphere that mediates temporal perception, is indirect and results from research that has been done with this set-up (Bakker, 1967a; Groenendaal & Bakker, 1971). Above-average and below-average readers (within a group of learning-disturbed and also within a group of normal children) appear to differ in achievements when temporal sequences of meaningful (i.e. nameable) figures are presented to them and when subsequently they will have to indicate which figure was presented first and which next. No group differences, however, occur where sequences of meaningless (i.e. unnameable) figures are concerned.

The procedure that was used is comparable with that of Hirsch & Sherrick and Efron, on the understanding that in our investigation a reconstruction-method was applied in view of the fact that meaningless figures cannot be labelled. Furthermore, 4 stimuli per series were presented instead of 2, and the ISIs were also longer than in Efron's investigation. But just as with this author the place of each item in a series was explicitly asked for.

Now, temporal perception of meaningful figures appears to be related with reading ability, whereas perception of meaningless figures is not. These results may be interpreted in such a way that the correlation between temporal perception of meaningful figures and reading is attributed to both (verbal) processes being mediated left-cerebrally. The absence of a relation between temporal perception of meaningless figures and reading may be caused by the fact that nonverbal processes (temporal perception of meaningless figures) are mediated right-cerebrally and verbal processes (reading) left-cerebrally.

In short, there appears to be reason to assume that a verbal moment was present in the tasks which Efron presented to his *S*s. His conclusion about the part played by the speech hemisphere in the assimilation of temporal processes can be viewed in the light of this verbal participation.

Therefore Efron's results are not conflicting with the evidence resulting from other research that it is not the temporal perception but the *temporal perception of something* that is lateralized cerebrally. Which part of the cerebrum is dominant depends on the 'substance' which is ordered in time, and not on the question whether temporal processes do or do not play any part (Bakker, 1970a). Left- *vs.* right-cerebral points (among other things) to differentiations along the line verbal-nonverbal and not to the distinction temporal-nontemporal.

5. PERSONAL RESEARCH

By means of two recent experiments in our laboratory the hypothesis was tested that asymmetry of temporal perception depends on the fact whether the stimuli are verbal or nonverbal in nature.

Seventy-two boys, 24 seven-year-olds and 24 nine-year-olds of normal primary schools, as well as 24 nine-year-olds of a school for learning-disturbances (clinic sample) participated in the first experiment. All groups were matched on IQ, the 9-year-old normal and learning-disturbed boys according to age and the 7-year-old normal and 9-year-old learning-disturbed boys according to reading ability.

Stimulation was tactile. Out of sight 2 or 3 fingers of each hand were stimulated in temporal succession by a slight, but clearly perceptible touch (stimulus duration and ISI about 1 sec. each). Ten series were presented to each hand. The hand-sequence was determined at random. For the sake of the response the two hands were drawn on a sheet of paper. After each series S had to indicate on the drawing which fingers were stimulated and in what order. An incorrect rendering of the sequence was considered an error. So a maximum of 10 points per hand could be scored.*

As it is here a matter of temporal perception without verbal participation, the prediction was that the left hand gives better performances than the right hand (dominance of the right hemisphere).

The *left minus right* differences are calculated per S and the mean differences have been rendered graphically in Fig. 18. In conformity with the hypothesis all groups show better performances with the left hand, although the left minus right differences are significant only with the 9-year-old normal boys ($t = 1.74$; $df = 23$; $p < .05$).

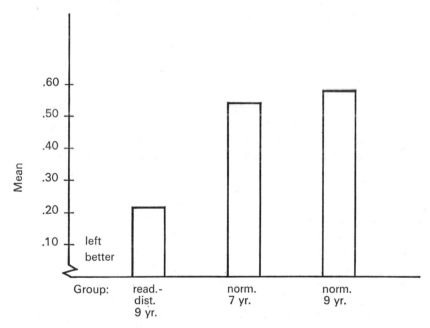

Fig. 18.   *Mean left minus right score with finger ordering by groups.*

---

* For a more detailed description of method and procedure of the two experiments the reader may be referred to Krul, Bakker & Hoekstra (in preparation).

That the oldest group shows the greatest differences is probably due to increasing cerebral lateralization with age (Satz & Sparrow, 1970). The data suggest that the clinic sample is retarded in cerebral lateralization by more than 2 years. For the mean difference-score of this group is smaller than that of the 7-year-old normal boys.

Another variable connected with cerebral dominance is hand preference. The right-handed boys (100% right-handed) appeared to obtain a mean difference-score of $+.60$, which is significant ($t = 1.94$; $df = 38$; $p < .05$). Those who are not right-handed (left- and not fully right-handed) had a mean difference-score of $+.29$, which is not significant ($t = .91$; $df = 32$; $p > .10$).

The relation with age and hand preference make it probable that in most cases nonverbal tactile-temporal processes are right-cerebrally mediated.

In the second experiment 80 children participated, 40 seven-year-olds and 40 nine-year-olds, 20 boys and 20 girls of each age.

The children, all from a normal primary school, were all right-handed.

Ten seven-year-olds (5 boys and 5 girls) and 10 nine-year-olds (6 boys and 4 girls) were trained in the numbering of the fingers, in such a way that each finger could quickly be vocally indicated by its number. The rest of the children, 30 seven-year-olds (15 boys and 15 girls) and 30 nine-year-olds (15 boys and 15 girls), were given no verbal training. The children were assigned at random to the verbal and nonverbal condition.

The procedure of the nonverbal condition was exactly the same as the one of the first experiment. So 2 or 3 fingers of each hand were touched in temporal succession, out of sight. On a response card, on which the two hands were drawn, S had to indicate in correct order which fingers had been stimulated.

Since the task is temporal-nonverbal in nature better performances of the left hand were expected.

Children under the verbal condition had to name the stimulated fingers in correct order by means of the numbers belonging to them. The rest of the procedure was similar to that of the nonverbal condition. Since this task is temporal-verbal in nature better performances of the right hand (left hemisphere dominance) were expected.

For the second experiment other Ss were used than for the first one.

The *left minus right* differences were again calculated per S. A positive score indicates better performances by the left hand, a negative score better performances by the right hand. The mean difference-scores have been rendered in Fig. 19. The nine-year-old Ss show a significant left-hand dominance under the nonverbal condition ($t = 1.96$; $df = 29$; $p < .05$)

and a significant right-hand dominance under the verbal condition ($t =$ $= 3.87$; $df = 9$; $p < .005$). At the age of seven the difference-scores do not significantly differ from zero.

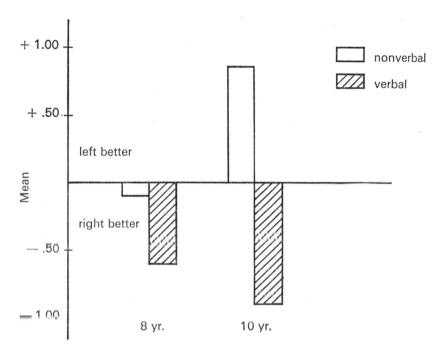

Fig. 19. *Mean left minus right score with finger ordering by age and experimental condition.*

The results under the nonverbal condition confirm those of the first experiment. A comparison of the results under the verbal and nonverbal condition confirms the hypothesis that the perception of temporal order is mediated left- or right-cerebrally, as it concerns the temporal order of either verbal or nonverbal stimuli.

6. THEORETICAL CONSIDERATIONS

'The word-order, a lingual relation, is purely lingual, and at the same time it is a manifestation of time in the lingual sphere. This characterizes each occurring of time in the modal sphere: it always indicates that time is

completely and perfectly modalized: we discover time in the modal sphere as a modal phenomenon, which is nonetheless recognizable as a manifestation of time*. That time in the physical sphere is a wholly physical phenomenon is not at all astonishing. It is a physical relation there. In the lingual sphere it is a lingual relation. And in the arithmetic sphere it is an arithmetic relation. And so on'. (Popma, 1965, p. 37. transl.)

Discussing succession and temporal order is discussing time. Time is recognizable as a relation. A relation is a relation of something, in its generality, of events.

Events are not all of the same order. Thus there are physical, biotic, psychic, lingual and esthetic events, and events otherwise qualified. A lingually qualified event, for instance, is a word, a sentence. Tones, lines, points, on the other hand, are not lingually qualified.

Events of different natures are mutually non-reducible, but not mutually independent. Speech is lingually qualified and the conception that speech may be sufficiently explained as a pattern of muscular movements is a biologistic misconception. It is true, however, that speech presupposes, among other things, the functioning of muscles.

Time itself is not an event, but a relation of events, regardless of their nature. Time occurs within all qualifications (modalities) and is therefore not a privilege of either lingual events or physical events or whatever events. In speech, time is among other things discovered as a sequence of phonemes, and in motion physical time manifests itself.

Time as a relation of events is determined by the nature of these events: psychic time is not the same as physical time. When a child is about to be born the clock may indicate that the doctor is 5 minutes late (physical time), but according to the 'psychic clock' it is possible that the period of waiting had lasted an 'eternity'. So it is sensible to speak of physical, biotic, psychic, lingual time, etc. All times are relations so that for instance the physical time is a physical relation and the lingual time is a lingual relation.

All differently qualified times are rooted in the one cosmic time. This time, however, is not accessible for empiric investigation.

The spectrum of colours at one side of the prism is closely connected with the one band of light at the other side. The same holds good for the modal times and the cosmic time. And just as blue and red are not identical, so the physical and lingual time are not identical times.

---

* With the words mode and modal one should not think in this case of sensory modes, etc. Its meaning here will become clear from what follows.

In specialized investigations it is therefore not useful to speak of *the* time and *the* temporal order *as such*. What one is dealing with in such an investigation is no more than an *aspect* of time in reality. If one should neglect this it is easy to slide into modalism (overrating of an aspect of reality).

With Efron (1963) there is rather a twofold threat of temporalism (overrating of time). It is no doubt true that time, especially as succession and temporal order, plays an important part in language. Language without succession is no language in the sense of intelligibility. This does not, however, alter the fact that time is only a relation conception. Language-time relates language-events, so that language and time are not identical.

The first threat of temporalism in Efron occurs when he inclines to identify language with language-time (probably partly because the difference between language-time and *the* time is neglected). This becomes evident wherever it is suggested that a disturbance in language is identical to a disturbance in (language-)time. 'When the speech rate exceeds the capacity of the (aphasic, D.J.B.) patient to properly sequence, complete failure of communication might result on the receptive side. If this view is correct we should not look upon the aphasias as unique disorders of language but rather as an inevitable consequence of a primary defect in temporal analysis – in placing a "time-label" upon incoming data' (p. 418).

An aphasia should therefore be considered as a primary defect in the functioning of time, and not as a unique disorder of language. Thus aphasia may be equated with defective functioning of time. Here the danger is imminent that language is considered as a manifestation of temporal functioning.

In the earlier quotation (Introduction) from Bannatyne (1966, p. 198) we can detect the same inclination: '... I would go so far as to say that a specific language disability could be redefined as a specific auditory sequencing disability'. Substitute a few words and it says that language may be redefined as an auditory sequencing process. This is exactly what Bannatyne states with some caution one line earlier: 'It is surprising how many teachers and educational authorities ... forget that language is almost entirely an auditory sequencing process.' Language, however, is not a little more but much more than a sequencing process. Language for instance takes also space besides time.

Another threat of temporalism seems to be more serious and occurs wherever language-time is more or less identified with *the* time. Identified more or less, for Efron is not altogether consistent. He correctly states that with a disturbance in what he calls temporal sequencing or temporal analysis, other functions apart from language get disturbed as well. In connection with these other functions he mentions the 'higher' or 'cognitive' functions, such as thinking. Time, however, plays a part not only in these functions. In such a complex skill as walking, for instance, temporal sequencing is an important moment. A temporal disturbance *as such* will have consequences for all functions and so for behaviour in its totality.

Now, the results of lesions in the speech hemisphere (where language-time is represented) are not so far-reaching, fortunately. Such lesions do not lead to a temporal disturbance, but to difficulties in the assimilation of language-time.

How striking but also how event-selective the influence of time is appears from a number of case-studies by Luria (1968). 'We have had numerous occasions to observe patients in whom lesions in the premotor zone of the cortex produced complete inability to form a well automatized motor habit, and who, for example, were unable to beat out a rhythm such as −− ··· −− ··· However, if we added speech to the implementation of this task and asked the patient to dictate to himself, "One, two-one, two, three" or to say to himself, "strong, strong, weak, weak, weak" or even to give himself auxiliary symbolic support by means of speech (...) the task, based on the system of directive connections arising on the basis of speech, was successfully achieved' (p. 362).

Were those patients disturbed in temporal functioning? This cannot be stated so simply. If it were true the imitation of the rhythmic patterns by words would not have been possible. It is evident that with these patients the functioning of one or more modal manifestations of time has been disturbed. But in any case with these patients it was not language-time.

So theoretical analysis and empirical investigation furnish evidence of the continuity of Efron's and Milner's results. What they demonstrated respectively is that time relations of lingual events are mediated left-cerebrally and those of nonlingual events right-cerebrally.

VIII. Cerebral lateralization of the TOP-reading interaction

The temporal perception of verbal and of verbal codifiable stimuli is mediated by the language hemisphere (Efron, 1963). No less does this apply to a language process like reading. Said temporal perception and reading consequently possess the same substratum, by which the TOP-reading relation found is to be explained.

Other variables can be mentioned that correlate with reading, possibly because they share with reading the same (mostly the left) hemisphere as cortical mediation area. With specific reading disturbances Gerstmann symptoms are often found to occur, such as left-right confusion, calculation difficulties, finger-differentiation problems and impairment in form perception. The coinciding of these phenomena with reading disturbances may be attributed to a developmental lag in the functioning of the whole left hemisphere (Satz & Sparrow, 1970; Sparrow & Satz, 1970). This lag, according to them, is due to the fact that the motor, the somato-sensory and the language functions respectively lateralize late. According to Satz & Sparrow specific reading disturbances at relatively young ages are therefore found to coincide with motor and somato-sensory defects and at later ages with language difficulties. At this point one should indeed speak of phenomena *coinciding* since *direct* causal relations are probably out of the question in most cases. The processes underlying the Gerstmann signs will in general not bring about reading disturbances but accompany them owing to an insufficient development of either substratum (the left hemisphere).

As was stated earlier reading and temporal perception of verbal stimuli are both controlled by the left hemisphere. On merely this ground TOP-reading relations may be expected.

But there is more. Temporal order is to reading as a part is to a whole. Spreen (1970) rightly notes that with investigations into the relations between the perception of temporal order and reading it is the nature of the reading process itself that is really studied. Between the perception of temporal order and reading there is a direct causal relation. A disturbed

87

temporal perception will result into a disturbed reading process. A similar correlation exists between temporal order and spoken language.

There are, however, indications that this functional interaction of temporal order on the one hand and reading and spoken language on the other has not existed from the beginning. The partial aspects of language appear to develop at different moments. The child uses phonemes at an early stage, at first especially vowels and subsequently also consonants. Not until later will the phonemes be woven into words and later still the words into sentences (McCarthy, 1954). So succession and temporal order are gradually going to play a part in spoken language. A similar development is seen in the learning of written language a few years later. Reading and writing of individual letters is not so difficult. Synthesizing letters into a word and words into a sentence, however, is more difficult.

The 'primitive' aspects of spoken and written language respectively are apparently developed first. They disappear last with disturbances. Reading-disturbed children hardly able to read a sentence are in many cases able to name letters.

Not until later are temporal operations applied to language symbols. This process requires a conscious activity from the individual in which the ordering in time has explicit attention.

The neurophysiological conditions for language acquisition may be found in the lateral differentiation of cerebral functions that increases with age. The language functions come gradually under control of the left hemisphere. The developments of spoken and written language that were described give rise to the assumption that this specialization takes place in stages. First spoken language is represented unilaterally, and then written language. Further the 'primitive' aspects of both languages – the enumeration and naming of verbal symbols – are first represented unilaterally, and then the temporal aspects follow. When naming and ordering of writing symbols are both controlled by the left hemisphere it is possible to speak of a critical period for temporal operations in the field of written language.

Of this phase the TOP-reading relation that was found is presumably a reflection.

The question then is how with this presumption a number of results are to be explained.

First the fact that the TOP-reading relation with girls occurs at a lower age than with boys. Consequently in Ch. V the critical period for TOP-reading interaction with girls was considered to occur earlier than with boys. Is it now possible to assume that the neurophysiological conditions for this interaction are present with girls at an earlier age than with boys? Two arguments confirming this question can be given. In the first place language appears to develop earlier and more quickly with girls than with boys (McCarthy, 1954). Secondly a similar sex difference with regard to the age at which language lateralizes has become evident from a number of investigations with dichotic and monaural listening techniques (Bakker, 1970; Bryden, 1970). On the ground of these data it may be assumed that the lateral specialization for the ordering of writing symbols occurs earlier with girls than with boys.

Another result of our investigation is that the TOP-reading relation does no longer occur after a certain age; at least no longer with girls of the age of 7 or more. On the ground of this result an upper limit of the critical period for TOP-reading interaction had to be assumed. But one cannot assume that at a certain moment reading takes place without temporal perception, although the reading process and the temporal perception in it are subject to changes. In the early learning-to-read process temporal operations are found to occur in the field of written symbols as conscious activities in which the ordering in time gets explicit attention. Also with reading-disturbed children the attention is continually focused on the ordering of graphemes and phonemes. In later phases of normal reading temporal perception can no longer be considered as an explicit operation. Ordering is a process that has become implicit in reading.

The tests for the perception and retention of temporal order were of the VE-type in our investigations. The location of each item in a series had to be indicated explicitly. Tests of this type simulate to a high degree the early learning-to-read process with its explicit ordering of writing symbols. It was stated earlier that reading on an advanced level is simulated well with a test of the VI-type, in which temporal series are imitated.

The fact that with older girls no TOP-reading relation could be determined may therefore be attributed to the type of test (VE) that was used. It is to be expected that with a test of the VI-type a TOP-relation will be found with normal readers of an older age.

Thus a critical period for TOP-reading *interaction*, with progressive cerebral lateralization of language functions as a neurophysiological correlate, appears to explain sufficiently the TOP-reading *relation* found and the influences of age and sex occurring with this relation.

These results of research and theoretical analysis may be important for understanding the learning-to-read process and for the development of training programmes.

If the critical period for TOP-reading interaction appears with girls earlier than with boys, this could be a reason for keeping the starting-age of the actual reading instruction variable. This moment is chosen too early if the organism is not yet mature for it, a risk that applies more to boys than to girls. This is perhaps one of the reasons why reading disturbances occur more frequently with boys than with girls.

Once a child appears to be reading-disturbed one may think it necessary to apply training programmes. Nowadays one may even have the disposal of complete teaching programmes (e.g. Dumont & Kok, 1970). It is to be recommended that such programmes take the stages of development of the child into account. In order to promote reading ability it may be required first to create the necessary conditions for this. It is not inconceivable that with disturbed children the training of reading ability works even in the wrong way. When the organism is not mature for it, one is sowing into infertile soil.

And here is harmful what is no good.

The creation of conditions implies that one is stimulating a good introduction to actual reading. This may involve an examination of spoken language of the child and a correction of it if necessary. '... reading is far more intimately related to a *necessary* substrata of normal oral language development than we presently perceive' (Brown, 1970). But dependent on the nature of the developmental disturbance the promotion of a good introduction may as well imply taking altogether different measures. After all, reading includes more than just temporal aspects.

All possible measures, however, are to little avail if the organism is not mature for it. Unless they further the maturation itself.

Hardly anything is known about these problems. A challenge for a developmental and educational neuropsychology.

References

Bakker, D.J. Een onderzoek naar de etiologische factoren bij leesstoornissen. Unpublished report, Pedological Institute Research Department, Amsterdam, 1964.

Bakker, D.J. Leesstoornissen: Een foutenanalyse. *Nederlands tijdschrift voor de psychologie*, 1965, 20, 173-183.

Bakker, D.J. Sensory dominance in normal and backward readers. *Perceptual and motor skills*, 1966, 23, 1055-1058.

Bakker, D.J. Temporal order, meaningfulness, and reading ability. *Perceptual and motor skills*, 1967a, 24, 1027–1030.

Bakker, D.J. Sensory dominance and reading ability. *Journal of communication disorders*, 1967b, 1, 316–318.

Bakker, D.J. Left-right differences in auditory perception of verbal and non-verbal material by children. *Quarterly journal of experimental psychology*, 1967c, 19, 334–336.

Bakker, D.J. Ear-asymmetry with monaural stimulation. *Psychonomic science*, 1968, 12, 62.

Bakker, D.J. Ear-asymmetry with monaural stimulation: Task influences. *Cortex*, 1969, 5, 36-42.

Bakker, D.J. Ear-asymmetry with monaural stimulation: Relations to lateral dominance and lateral awareness. *Neuropsychologia*, 1970a, 8, 103-117.

Bakker, D.J. Temporal order perception and reading retardation. In D.J. Bakker & P. Satz (Eds.), *Specific reading disability, advances in theory and method*. Rotterdam: Rotterdam University Press, 1970b, 81–96.

Bakker, D.J. & Boeijenga, J.A. Ear-order effects on ear-asymmetry with monaural stimulation. *Neuropsychologia*, 1970, 8, 385–386.

Bannatyne, A.D. The color phonics system. In J. Money (Ed.), *The disabled reader: Education of the dyslexic child*. Baltimore: Johns Hopkins Press, 1966, 193–214.

Belmont, L. & Birch, H.G. The intellectual profile of retarded readers. *Perceptual and motor skills*, 1966, 22, 787–816.

Benton, A.L., Van Allen, M.W., & Fogel, M.L. Temporal orientation in cerebral disease. *The journal of nervous and mental disease*, 1964, 139, 110–119.

Berk, T.J.C. De betekenis van enige aspecten van de tijd voor psychotherapie. *Nederlands tijdschrift voor de psychologie*, 1965, 20, 419–451.

Birch, H.G. Dyslexia and the maturation of visual function. In J. Money (Ed.), *Reading disability: Progress and research needs in dyslexia*. Baltimore: Johns Hopkins Press, 1962, 161–177.

Birch, H.G. & Belmont, L. Auditory-visual integration in normal and retarded readers. *American journal of orthopsychiatry*, 1964, 34, 852–861.

Birch, H.G. & Belmont, L. Auditory-visual integration, intelligence and reading ability in school children. *Perceptual and motor skills*, 1965, 20, 295–305.

Blalock, H.M. *Causal inferences in nonexperimental research*. Chapel Hill: The University of North Carolina Press, 1964.

Blank, M. & Bridger, W.H. Deficiencies in verbal labeling in retarded readers. *American journal of orthopsychiatry*, 1966, 36, 840-847.

Blank, M., Weider, S. & Bridger, W.H. Verbal deficiencies in abstract thinking in early reading retardation. *American journal of orthopsychiatry*, 1968, 38, 823-834.

Brown, E. The bases of reading acquisition. *Reading research quarterly*, 1970, 6, 49-74.

Bryden, M.P. Laterality effects in dichotic listenings: Relations with handedness and reading ability in children. *Neuropsychologia*, 1970, 8, 443-450.

Caldwell, B.M. The usefulness of the critical period hypothesis in the study of filiative behavior. *Merrill-Palmer quarterly of behavior and development*, 1962, 8, 229-242.

Chase, R.A. In C.H. Millikan & F.L. Darley (Eds.), *Brain mechanisms underlying speech and language*. New York: Grune & Stratton, 1967, p. 135 ff.

Clark, L., Knowles, J.B. & Maclean, A. The effects of method of recall on performance in the dichotic listening task. *Canadian journal of psychology*, 1970, 24, 194-198.

Clements, G.R. An abbreviated form of the Wechsler Intelligence Scale for Children. *Journal of consulting psychology*, 1965, 29, 92.

Cohen, J. *Psychological time in health and disease*. Springfield: Thomas, 1967.

Conners, C.K., Kramer, K., & Guerra, F. Auditory synthesis and dichotic listening in children with learning disabilities. *The journal of special education*, 1969, 3, 163-170.

DeHirsch, K., Jansky, J.J. & Langford, W.S. *Predicting reading failure: A preliminary study*. New York: Harper & Row, 1966.

De Wit, J., & Bakker, D.J. Leesstoornissen. In J. De Wit, H. Bolle, & R. Jessurun Cardozo-Van Hoorn (Eds.), *Psychologen over het kind* II. Groningen: Wolters-Noordhoff, 1971, 177-192.

Dimond, S.J. Hemisphere function and immediate memory. *Psychonomic science*, 1969, 16, 111-112.

Drenth, P.J.D., Petrie, J.F., & Bleichrodt, N. *Amsterdamse Kinder Intelligentie Test*. Amsterdam: Swets & Zeitlinger, 1968.

Dumont, J.J., & Kok, J.F.W. *Curriculum schoolrijpheid*, deel 1. 's-Hertogenbosch, Holland: Malmberg, 1970.

Edwards, A.E., & Auger, R. The effect of aphasia on the perception of precedence. *Proceedings of the 73rd annual convention of the american psychological association*, 1965, 207-208.

Efron, R. Temporal perception, aphasia, and déjà vu. *Brain*, 1963a, 86, 403-424.

Efron, R. The effect of handedness on the perception of simulaneity and temporal order. *Brain*, 1963b, 86, 261-284.

Efron, R. The effect of stimulus intensity on the perception of simultaneity in right- and left-handed cases. *Brain*, 1963c, 86, 285-294.

Efron, R. In C.H. Millikan & F.L. Darley (Eds.), *Brain mechanisms underlying speech and language.*, New York: Grune & Stratton, 1967, p. 30ff.

Eisenberg, L. The epidemiology of reading retardation and a program for preventive intervention. In J. Money (Ed.), *The disabled reader: Education of the dyslexic child*. Baltimore: Johns Hopkins Press, 1966, 3-20.

Fedio, P., & Mirsky, A.F. Selective intellectual deficits in children with temporal lobe or centrencephalic epilepsy. *Neuropsychologia*, 1969, 7, 287-300.

Ferguson, G. A. *Statistical analysis in psychology and education.* New York: McGraw-Hill, 1966.

Fokkema, S. D. Attributen-correlatie en afhankelijkheidsrelatie in de psychologische research. *Nederlands tijdschrift voor de psychologie,* 1967, 22, 568–582.

Fossen, J. M. De invloed van kleur op het waarnemen en onthouden van temporele sekwenties. Unpublished report, Pedological Institute Research Department, Amsterdam, 1969.

Fraisse, P. *The psychology of time.* New York: Harper & Row, 1963.

Furth, H. G., & Youniss, J. Sequence learning: Perceptual implications in the acquisition of language. In W. Wathen-Dunn (Ed.), *Models for the perception of speech and visual form.* Cambridge, Massachusetts: The M.I.T. Press, 1967, 344–353.

Gattegno, C. The morphologico-algebraic approach to teaching reading. In J. Money (Ed.), *The disabled reader: Education of the dyslexic child.* Baltimore: Johns Hopkins Press, 1966, 175–189.

Gengel, R. W., & Hirsh, I. J. Temporal order: The effect of single versus repeated presentations, practice, and verbal feedback. *Perception & psychophysics,* 1970, 7, 209–211.

Goldstone, S., & Goldfarb, J. L. The perception of time by children. In A. H. Kidd & J. L. Rivoire (Eds.), *Perceptual development in children.* New York: International Universities Press, 1966, 445–486.

Groenendaal, H. A., & Bakker, D. J. The part played by mediation processes in the retention of temporal sequences by two reading groups. *Human development,* 1971, 14, 62–70.

Halliday, A. M., & Mingay, R. Retroactive raising of a sensory threshold by a contra-lateral stimulus. *Quarterly journal of experimental psychology,* 1961, 13, 1–11.

Hays, W. L. *Statistics for psychologists.* New York: Holt, Rinehart & Winston, 1963

Hirsh, I. J. Auditory perception of temporal order. *The journal of the acoustical society of america,* 1959, 31, 759–767.

Hirsh, I. J. & Fraisse, P. Simultanéité et succession de stimuli hétérogènes. *Année psychologique,* 1964, 64, 1–19.

Hirsh, I. J., & Sherrick, C. E. Perceived order in different sense modalities. *Journal of experimental psychology,* 1961, 62, 423–432.

Holmes, H. L. Disordered perception of auditory sequences in aphasia. Unpublished thesis, Harvard University, 1965.

Hugenholtz, P. Th. *Tijd en tijdsvormen.* Zutphen, Holland: Ruys, 1938.

Hugenholtz, P. Th. *Tijd en creativiteit.* Amsterdam: Noord-Hollandse Uitgeversmij., 1959.

Kahn, D. & Birch, H. G. Development of auditory-visual integration and reading achievement. *Perceptual and motor skills,* 1968, 27, 459–468.

Keogh, B. K., & Smith, C. E. Visuo-motor ability for school prediction: A seven-year study. *Perceptual and motor skills,* 1967, 25, 101–110.

Kimura, D. Left-right differences in the perception of melodies. *Quarterly journal of experimental psychology,* 1964, 16, 355–358.

Kimura, D. Functional asymmetry of the brain in dichotic listening. *Cortex,* 1967, 3, 163–178.

Kinsbourne, M. & Warrington, E. K. Developmental factors in reading and writing backwardness. In J. Money (Ed.), *The disabled reader: Education of the dyslexic child.* Baltimore: Johns Hopkins Press, 1966, 59–72.

93

Krul, P., Bakker, D.J. & Hoekstra, F. *Left-right differences in tactile-temporal perception of uncodified and verbally codified fingers by children.* In preparation.

Leene, J.G. & Bakker, D.J. Mistakes made in reading and dictation by above-average and below-average temporal order perceivers. Unpublished report, Pedological Institute Research Department, Amsterdam, 1969.

Lovell, K., & Gorton, A. A study of some differences between backward and normal readers of average intelligence. *British journal of educational psychology*, 1968, 38, 240–248.

Lowe, A.D. & Campbell, R.A. Temporal discrimination in aphasoid and normal children. *Journal of speech and hearing research*, 1965, 8, 313–314.

Luria, A.R. The directive function of speech in development and dissolution, part II. In R.C. Oldfield & J.C. Marshall (Eds.), *Language.* Harmondsworth, England: Penguin Books, 1968, 353–365.

Lyle, J.G. & Goyen, J. Performance of retarded readers on the WISC and educational tests. *Journal of abnormal psychology*, 1969, 74, 105–112.

Malone, R.L. Temporal ordering and speech identification abilities. *The journal of speech and hearing research*, 1967, 10, 542–548.

Masland, R.L. In C.H. Millikan & F.L. Darley (Eds.), *Brain mechanisms underlying speech and language.* New York: Grune & Stratton, 1967, p. 141ff.

McCarthy, D. Language development in children. In L. Carmichael (Ed.), *Manual of child psychology.* New York: Wiley, 1954, 492–630. Michon, J.A. De perceptie van duur. *Nederlands tijdschrift voor de psychologie*, 1965, 20, 391–418.

Milner, B. Laterality effects in audition. In V.B. Mountcastle (Ed.), *Interhemispheric relations and cerebral dominance.* Baltimore: Johns Hopkins Press, 1962, 177–195.

Milner, B. Brain mechanisms suggested by studies of temporal lobes. In C.H. Millikan & F.L. Darley (Eds.), *Brain mechanisms underlying speech and language.* New York: Grune & Stratton, 1967, 122–145.

Monsees, E.K. Temporal sequence and expressive language disorders. *Exceptional children*, 1968, 35, 141–147.

Muller, F. & Bakker, D.J. Temporal order perception and reading ability. Unpublished report, Pedological Institute Research Department, Amsterdam, 1968.

Orme, J.E. *Time, experience and behaviour.* London: Iliffe Books, 1969.

Ornstein, R.E. *On the experience of time.* Harmondsworth, England: Penguin Books, 1969.

Pelle, P.G. De statistische verwerking van toenamescores. *Nederlands tijdschrift voor de psychologie*, 1967, 22, 277–288.

Piaget, J. *The child's conception of time.* London: Routledge & Kegan Paul, 1969.

Popma, K.J. *Nadenken over de tijd.* Amsterdam: Buyten & Schipperheyn, 1965.

Renshaw, S. The errors of cutaneous localization and the effect of practice on the localizing movement in children and adults. *Journal of genetic psychology*, 1930, 38, 223–238.

Rosenbusch, M.H., & Gardner, D.B. Reproduction of visual and auditory rhythm patterns by children. *Perceptual and motor skills*, 1968, 26, 1271–1276.

Ross, B.M., & Youniss, J. Ordering of nonverbal items in children's recognition memory. *Journal of experimental child psychology*, 1969, 8, 20–32.

94

Sanders, A.F. *De psychologie van de informatieverwerking.* Arnhem, Holland: Van Loghum Slaterus, 1967.

Sapir, S.G. Sex differences in perceptual motor development. *Perceptual and motor skills*, 1966, 22, 987–992.

Satz, P., & Sparrow, S.S. Specific developmental dyslexia: A theoretical formulation. In D.J. Bakker & P. Satz (Eds.), *Specific reading disability, advances in theory and method.* Rotterdam: Rotterdam University Press, 1970, 17–40.

Schulhoff, C., & Goodglass, H. Dichotic listening, side of brain injury and cerebral dominance. *Neuropsychologia*, 1969, 7, 149–160.

Scott, J.P. Critical periods in the development of social behavior in puppies. *Psychosomatic medicine*, 1958, 20, 42–54.

Senf, G.M. Development of immediate memory for bisensory stimuli in normal children and children with learning disorders. *Developmental psychology*, 1969, 6, prt. 2.

Shankweiler, D. Defects in recognition and reproduction of familiar tunes after unilateral temporal lobectomy. Paper presented at 37th annual meeting, eastern psychological association, New York, 1966[a].

Shankweiler, D. Effects of temporal-lobe damage on perception of dichotically presented melodies. *Journal of comparative and physiological psychology*, 1966[b], 62, 115–119.

Sluckin, W. *Early learning in man and animal.* London: George Allen and Unwin, 1970.

Sparrow, S.S., & Satz, P. Dyslexia, laterality and neuropsychological development. In D.J. Bakker & P. Satz (Eds.), *Specific reading disability, advances in theory and method.* Rotterdam: Rotterdam University Press, 1970, 41–60.

Spellacy, F.J. Lateral preferences in the identification of patterned stimuli. *The journal of the acoustical society of america*, 1970, 47, 574–578.

Spier, J.M. *Tijd en eeuwigheid.* Kampen, Holland: Kok, 1953.

Spreen, O. Postcript: Review and outlook. In D.J. Bakker & P. Satz (Eds.), *Specific reading disability, advances in theory and method.* Rotterdam: Rotterdam University Press, 1970, 1–15.

Spreen, O., Spellacy, F.J., & Reid, J.R. The effect of interstimulus interval and intensity on ear-asymmetry for nonverbal stimuli in dichotic listening. *Neuropsychologia*, 1970, 8, 245–250.

Stamback, M. Le problème du rhytme dans le développement de l'enfant et dans les dyslexies d'évolution. *Enfance*, 1951, 5, 480–493.

Stark, J. A comparison of the performance of aphasic children on three sequencing tests. *Journal of communication disorders*, 1967, 1, 31–34.

Van Allen, M.W., Benton, A.L., & Gordon, M.C. Temporal discrimination in brain-damaged patients. *Neuropsychologia*, 1966, 4, 159–167.

Van der Horst, L. Het amnestisch symptomencomplex. In L. Van der Horst, *Anthropologische psychiatrie.* Amsterdam: Van Holkema & Warendorf, 1952, 243–260.

Van der Wissel, A. Spellingmoeilijkheden, minus-variant of dysorthografie? *Nederlands tijdschrift voor de psychologie*, 1963, 18, 13–42.

Van Meel, J.M. *Bedreigd denken.* Groningen: Wolters, 1968.

Van Meel, J.M., Vlek, C.A.J., & Bruijel, R.M. Some characteristics of visual information processing in children with learning difficulties. In D.J. Bakker & P. Satz (Eds.), *Specific reading disability, advances in theory and method.* Rotterdam: Rotterdam University Press, 1970, 97–114.

Von Wright, J.M. Cross-modal transfer and sensory equivalence — A review. Paper presented at the international congress of psychology, London, 1969.

95

Wallace, M., & Rabin, A.I. Temporal experience. *Psychological bulletin*, 1960, 57, 213–236.

White, S.H. Evidence for a hierarchical arrangement of learning processes. In L.P. Lipsitt & C.C. Spiker (Eds.), *Advances in child behavior and development*, Vol. 2. New York: Academic Press, 1965.

Wiegersma, S. *Leesvaardigheidstest*. Leiden, Holland: Nederlands Instituut voor Praeventieve Geneeskunde, 5, 1958.

Winer, B.J. *Statistical principles in experimental design*. New York: McGraw-Hill, 1962.

Wohlwill, J.F. From perception to inference: A dimension of cognitive development. In I.E. Sigel & F.H. Hooper (Eds.), *Logical thinking in children*. New York: Holt, Rinehart & Winston, 1968, 472–494.

Index

98